Eyes Can't See

Max J. Traughber-Crismon

Disclaimer:

This book was written to give those a voice who struggle with hidden disabilities. Awareness of this subject is the key for understanding how we are affected by these. I know that there are people out there that have experienced much more trauma than myself. The intent is that through the chapters of this book, people are more open to trauma and disabilities when they cannot see them.

I am no longer angry or hold resentment towards people who I have mentioned throughout. My goal is that this book will not only allow myself to heal, but those that also struggle with hidden disabilities.

Title Page

Disclaimer	pg. 2
Table of Context	pg. 3
Forward	pg. 4
The Yellow Chair	pg. 6
Product of a Generation	pg. 13
Silence Could Kill	pg. 34
War Guilt	pg. 44
Hot Iron	pg. 74
Change the Narrative	pg. 85
Corporate Throat Punch	pg. 97
Olive	pg. 117
On The Mound	pg. 128
Current State of Mind	pg. 151
A Therapist Take	pg. 159
Beyond The Cover	pg. 175
Acknowledgments	pg. 182
Thank You	pg. 183

Azlan Allen, Army Infantry Veteran, Airborne~

Discovering the Unseen - A Personal Voyage in "Eyes Can't See"

"Eyes Can't See" isn't just a book; it feels more like sitting down for a heart-to-heart with an old friend who's about to share their most intimate secrets. It's a deep dive into the often-overlooked world of hidden disabilities, told with the kind of honesty and warmth that makes you feel like you're part of the story.

For years, we've only heard half the story about disabilities—the part that's easy to see. But this book throws open the curtains on the other half, the silent struggles that don't always get the spotlight.

The author's own story is at the center of it all. It's a tale that stretches over forty years, filled with the kind of ups and downs that make you nod in recognition. They didn't always have the answers, but who does? Their journey of facing and embracing hidden challenges is relatable—it's about finding your voice, even if it takes a while.

But the book goes beyond just one person's experience. It's a collection of voices, each sharing their truth about living with an unseen disability, like a mosaic, with each piece telling a part of a larger story, and every story is told with raw, unfiltered emotion.

What makes this book so special is its honesty. It doesn't sugarcoat or tiptoe around the tough stuff. It's not about pointing fingers or living in the past. Instead, it's about understanding, growing, and looking at the world through a more empathetic lens.

"Eyes Can't See" is more than just a memoir. It's a rallying cry for all of us to open our eyes to the hidden struggles around us. It's an invitation to be part of a bigger conversation, one that acknowledges and respects the full range of human experiences.

As you turn each page, you're not just reading a book—you're joining a journey. A journey that promises to shake up how you see the world, touch your heart, and remind you that even the struggles we can't see are very, very real.

Welcome to the world of "Eyes Can't See," a journey that might just change the way you see everything.

The Yellow Chair

I confronted my mom about her contributions to my childhood trauma a few days before Thanksgiving in 2022. It wasn't some big intervention, there was no plan to it, and to be honest, at that point in time, I wasn't even sure I ever wanted to discuss it with her. But, it happened, like hitting a patch of black ice on a January road, and I was forced to slam the brakes or skate.

For the first time in my life, I didn't brake.

"He didn't tell you that he didn't want you to come with us because he is afraid of you," I heard my wife exclaim in the tone of voice that I knew only came with the red burn of her cheeks and the adrenaline rush of confrontation. She didn't confront others often, she is a self-proclaimed "people-pleaser", but when a situation arose where her boundaries were crossed, she erupted.

I was halfway down the stairs of our two-story, suburban home, after having spent the last fifteen minutes or so messing around with the kids upstairs. Meredith was downstairs with my parents, anxiously cleaning and entertaining, as she often did in the presence of my parents. She didn't like being left alone with my parents, mainly because she had a tumultuous history with my mom's passive aggressive commentary that seemed to arise mostly in my absence, and I don't remember exactly why I headed upstairs with the kids and left her alone with them, but neither of us thought much of it at the time. But when I heard Meredith's frustrated exclamation, I froze mid-stride before feeling the piercing laser gaze of both of my parents and wife.

It was like a scene out of a movie, where the teen girl gets a makeover and comes down the stairs for her "big reveal." Only, instead of a teen girl, I was a thirty-eight-year-old, six-foot-two-inch, 220 lb. man, and instead of a makeover, I was about to reveal years of emotional abuse at the hands of my parents.

With all of those eyes on me, I deflated. This isn't uncommon for me when faced with confrontation. I'm not like my wife. I don't confront anyone. When I am confronted, I transform into my younger self, my childhood self, a boy of just five or six. When it comes to fight or flight, I choose a third route: I freeze. My body goes numb, but my skin goes hot. So there I was, five years old, under the gaze of the parents who knew me then, and the wife who knows me now, like a deer in the path of a mountain lion. *What the hell did I just walk into?*

I looked at Meredith, and could see the relief on her face that I was here to support her through this argument that

I had no idea was happening downstairs, relief that so strongly juxtaposed from the cloud of panic that consumed me. For a beat that felt as long as the intro credits to *Star Wars*, no one said a word. Then finally, my mom said, "You're afraid of me?"

My mom is already tall, but her commanding presence makes her rival a Redwood. She, like my wife, doesn't fear confrontation, but hers is to the point of almost seeking it out as a hobby. Her years as a high school teacher and a social worker specializing in Child Protective Services had prepared her for just about any and all confrontation. However, she wasn't prepared for this one.

She stood there staring at me from the other side of our kitchen island, demanding a response that I had not been prepared to give. Sure, I had discussed at length how intimidated I was of my mom with my wife, to the point where talking about it was normal and comfortable with her, but no one else outside of that, most especially my mom and dad. But Meredith had opened Pandora's Box.

At this point, Meredith stood up to leave the room, clearly at her maximum threshold of what she felt obligated to be part of when it came to arguing with my parents. In a sense, as she passed me on the stairs, it was like she handed me an invisible baton. I had a choice to make. I could take the baton and charge forward through the race, or, I could drop it.

Without responding right away to my mom, and without saying a word to Meredith as she passed by me, I managed to unstick my feet from the stair they were plastered to, and crept forward, baton in hand. After all, this was my race, not hers.

In making the decision to walk down those stairs and meet my mom across the kitchen island, I made the choice to no longer stay as five-year-old Max at that moment. "Yes," I said to her as I found my trembling words. "I am afraid of you."

When I was about six years old, my mom was angry. I can't remember why my mother was mad that day. I never really knew why she got so mad. We were in our kitchen, a small yellow room. Banana yellow walls in a space the size of an average walk-in closet, stuffed with appliances the way a riverside is crammed with bears looking for lunch. She had something in her hand, it appeared to be a knife, or something that resembled a weapon to me, a six year-old. Whenever my mom was mad, I froze, or if possible, escaped. In this situation, I ran. I headed straight to my bedroom, my safe haven. I took the only route possible to get there, which was through the cramped dining room, across the 1930s wood flooring that creaked under my toe, scampering up the stairs. I felt the rough carpet beneath my feet as I headed to my room. My mom chased after me, the expression on her face seared into my mind. Her eyes were wide like an owl's, round and sinister. Her mouth was stretched into an eerie smile that was devoid of joy, like a Cheshire cat. Once in my room, I was cornered by those eyes and that smile. I hid behind a little yellow chair, my shield. That's all I can remember from that day.

    I often struggle to remember exactly how these types of situations played out. Details are fuzzy, but images in my mind are vivid. I remember how I felt and what I saw, but not so much what was said, or why. Trying to communicate these experiences to my mom, in that moment across the kitchen island, left me stumbling over my memories and words, as I often did. Yes, I was afraid of my mom. The Yellow Chair is just one story seared into my memory that has caused me lasting trauma. At that point, I had been made aware that my fear of my mom was the result of years of various situations that threatened my safety as a child, both emotionally and mentally. That much I knew, but how to address that with her was brand new territory for me, and I had no map to navigate it.

    At some point as I tipped the glass and let my memories flow, recalling these stories from my childhood that have built into this intense fear of her, my mom began to cry. She seemed to be hearing the words I was saying, but not understanding them. However, she was not denying them, either. When I had taken a breath to let the events that I had described sink in, she gathered herself and through her tears said, "So what, there was nothing good about your childhood then?"

Even though my mom makes no hesitation to say things that hurt others, she is, as this type of person always seems to be, extraordinarily sensitive. What this means for her, is that when threatened, she becomes defensive, and requires validation to balance out her negative feedback. Negative feedback wasn't often given to her, not because it was unwarranted, but because not many were willing to risk the repercussions. This situation was no different. She wanted to hear about all of her parenting successes to create a balance that softened the blow of my perspective. There were a lot of positive moments in my childhood, and with my mom. But in that moment, I needed her to hear me, to see me, and I needed her to acknowledge and take ownership for these events that happened, not just the positive ones.

Not all the experiences were trauma filled. We had family vacations and often spent time with my parents' friends, who had children also our age. I spent days out in the forests with my dad and grandma. Every once in a while we would visit family in the Portland, Oregon area and would explore what the area had to offer. There were good times in my childhood, but I needed her to acknowledge the other times in that moment.

Here we are, a few years later and that incident has never come back up. We move along like it never happened. I can only guess that she does not want to face what they had done to me. After that happened, I felt awful. It was good I was in therapy and had someone help me get through the emotions that I was thrust into. Feeling suffocated in my own thoughts about my past and trauma that I had experienced seemed to overwhelm me. In the next couple of years, I would work with my therapist trying to figure out how to cope with what happened. We worked on several things, but at the end, he said that I had to get everything out. My therapy springboarded me into writing this book. That single incident made me really dive deep into my past and unleash memories that I had suppressed. Family, sports, marriage, military and throughout my career I have faced abuse and discrimination. Here is my journey.

Product of a Generation

I grew up in a small rural town in Oregon. My days were filled with sports, school, and the outdoors. We experienced over 300 days of sun every year and the city very rarely had any clouds. Little did I know that people who I was surrounded by there, at that time of my life, would greatly influence my mental health as an adult.

Childhood for me at the time seemed extremely normal and most of my friends were all dealing with many of the childhood issues that I was dealing with. I was a big kid and always very strong. I was active, playing outside and working in the yards of my grandparents and other adults. People would see me playing football, baseball, and anything that I could get my hands on. What did they not see? They didn't see behind the facade of the young boy who seemed to be carefree.

As I have learned throughout my life, humans hardly ever make mistakes purposefully or willingly. As Maya Angelou said, "Do the best you can until you know better. Then when you know better, do better." These words couldn't be more true from my perspective. My parents loved me, but at times as a child, I had a hard time dealing with many of their behaviors.

My father is a hard-working blue-collar man who grew up and had issues of his own that he never dealt with. His father, who died when I was two years old, was a severe alcoholic. Back in my grandfather's generations, deals and sales pitches were done in the smoky room of a bar or on a golf course, especially in the real estate and insurance industries. During those times, drinking was a problem for many sales professionals and the drinking didn't stop at home.

My grandfather passed away when my dad was in his mid 20's and then a few short years later, my dad's only brother passed away from leukemia. My dad handled getting spanked (which was normal then) or yelled at by taking the beating and then staying out of the way. There were no apologies or acknowledgment of the abuse. Back in the '50s and '60s, spanking and yelling were part of the parental culture in many homes. I would hear stories of my dad putting padding in his pants so the spankings didn't hurt so bad.

My mother was in a different environment growing up, but one thing that my parents had in common was alcoholic fathers. Fortunately, I never knew my mother's father as an active alcoholic. My grandmother once told him that if he didn't stop drinking, she would leave him and make it clear to my mom and aunt that she was done. This also meant that I, as a baby, wouldn't have seen my grandfather. The following day he was in Alcoholics Anonymous and never drank again. Much of the damage was done though. My mom at the time was still in her mid 20's when I was born and had only been removed from her childhood for a handful of years. This was not enough time to process and understand her own childhood trauma. My mother grew up seeing my grandfather yell and scream at her and my aunt. I can only imagine it was similar to how I was treated as a child. There were days where they would hide and read in their rooms while my grandfather was in his "mood." My grandmother worked nights as a nurse, so she was not there while much of this had gone on.

    What happened after these children, my parents and relatives, were abused and how does this relate to hidden disabilities? My mom and dad grew up and became parents themselves. After years of mental abuse, my parents knew what they knew. Parenting, in all respects, is learned by watching who did it before you. Obviously, there are a variety of situations where this is different, but often you learn by watching.

Growing up, there were a few situations where I was terrified of my parents. I knew they loved me, but their anger caused such fear that I quickly learned coping mechanisms to deal with it. For a long time, I felt lucky that I was just yelled at and wasn't being physically abused. As I have gotten older, I realized that what I witnessed was extremely harmful to my future self.

Anxiety, depression, and post-traumatic stress disorder are all hidden disabilities that I have and they are the result of my trauma.

Post-trau-matic-stress dis-or-der

Noun

A condition of persistent mental and emotional stress occurring as a result of injury or severe psychological shock, typically involving disturbance of sleep and constant vivid recall of the experience, with dulled responses to others and to the outside world.

"She was undergoing counseling and psychotherapy after being diagnosed with post-traumatic stress disorder"

Anx-i-e-ty

Noun

A feeling of worry, nervousness, or unease, typically about an imminent event or something with an uncertain outcome,

De-pres-sion

Noun

A mental health condition characterized by feelings of severe despondency and dejection, typically also with feelings of inadequacy and guilt, often accompanied by lack of energy and disturbance of appetite and sleep.

"She was referred by a psychiatrist treating her for depression"

When I was young, five to seven years old, I saw something that no child should ever see. I saw my father pinning my mother up against a wall, at the end of a dark hallway, choking her. The image of my mom gasping for air, her face beat red and a shadow of my dad's 250 lbs. frame engulfing the space while small gasps of air squeezing from her thin lips will never leave my memory. I was terrified and had no idea what was going on. At that moment, the world turned dark. The fear overwhelmed and put me in a state of minor shock. This is one of the earliest memories I have from my childhood. My father and mother were always supposed to be there, providing a safe place, but at that moment, I felt invisible. People talk about an out of body experience, I believe that the feeling I had was exactly that. My young brain was in complete shock and felt more emotions than I had ever felt up until that point. From that point on, I made sure to steer clear of my father's anger and especially to stay away when he was drinking.

For many years, I thought about that moment. My perception of how to deal with relationship issues had completely changed. Now, as a man in my 40's, I can still see the image of my father choking my mother and I'm certain it is something that will forever be logged into my memory.

That night, my father came up to my room crying and telling me how sorry he was. Tears of sorrow fell from his cheek and his head in his hands lay on my mattress. I remember putting my hand on his street black hair and saying it was okay. My world had been turned upside down and I was now, as a young child, consoling my father who almost took the life of my mother. I can't remember a time before that where I ever saw him cry.

Roughly four or five years later, I experienced trauma that again was out of my control. My parents were fighting, and I was sitting in our dining room doing homework. Glass windows and a full China Hutch filled with precious plates and glasses surrounded me. In all honesty, I was probably looking out of the window, procrastinating. I remember trying to block out the fighting and yelling that I was witnessing. My dad was so loud, stomping around, that I thought there was an earthquake. We had experienced a few earthquakes in the past few years, so the trembling around the house brought me back. The windows rattled and the plates in the china hutch were on the verge of crashing down. My father came in and in a very loud voice said, "Who do you want to live with?!? Me or your mom!?!" His face bright red, body shaking with anger, fists clenched so tight no space could remain.

Since I was a scared kid, I trembled and said "you." What was I supposed to say at that moment? Fear, anxiety and everything that came with it hit me at once. I just wanted the screaming to stop. Confusion was only one of the emotions that I was experiencing at the time. Glued to the high back dining room chair, my back was pressed against the wood slats behind me. My fight, flight or freeze response on high alert. As I always did, I froze. Too scared to say anything other than what he wanted to hear.

In the upcoming months, my parents ended up going to a therapist and working on a few things. Although this helped, it didn't erase what I had witnessed. A distorted image of what I only knew as normal continued to follow. When people are young, we look at our parents/guardians for comfort and guidance. Anything other than that can cause tremendous harm. Again, if you know better, do better.

Their therapist wanted to have my sister and I go to some sessions as well. Family counseling, or counseling was brand new to me. We loaded up in the car and headed to our appointment. I had never been to a counselor before and was not at all sure why I was there or what was going to happen. During that time I had learned to just be quiet, stay hidden, stay out of the way. The counseling was a brand new experience. As a family we had to talk about how we felt and my sister and I were supposed to tell our parents how their behaviors were affecting us. Although I had no idea what anxiety was at that age, sitting in that room was the first time I remember feeling it. Dark wooden walls in the basement floor of the therapist's house seemed to suffocate me. The smell of an old book mixed with cleaning solvent filled my nose. Being told to tell my parents what they were doing seemed impossible. Fear is how I felt and in no way trusted that if I said anything, there wouldn't be a consequence. Looking back,

I should have opened the door to all of the things that were affecting me, but I was too afraid to say anything at all. Words didn't come easily that day and have slipped away from my memory. To this day, I never told them about how I felt during that time period.

What we experience as children, good or bad, stays with us for life. Some people will block out moments like these, but suppressing these feelings can cause much more damage. It has taken me over 30 years to start processing my childhood trauma, and that is just the start of it. My teenage years proved to be extremely challenging as well, but in many different ways. Adolescence is extremely tough for kids without trauma. Add in years of trauma; you are set up for some painful experiences ahead.

Heading into adolescence, my foundation and mental health were extremely unstable. Adolescence is hard enough on its own, but when you come into it with trauma, it can screw with the trajectory of your success. During this time in our life, the expectations grow immensely. Becoming an adult is the next step, but those who experience trauma often have a delay in advancing their personal development. Naturally, parts of their brain have been stalled while suppressing feelings of fear, anticipation of pain, and anxiety.

Not all PTSD comes from abuse. I found that out the hard way when I was about nine or ten years old. When I was a kid, I loved being at the pool on a hot summer day. The water, even to this day, calms me, which is probably why I chose the Navy for my military training, because there was nothing but water.

In my neighborhood there were tons of kids who liked going to the city pool. It had everything a kid would want—a slide, diving board, concession stand *and* a A&W Restaurant across the street. Often, after we were done swimming, we would walk over and get an ice cream or a root beer float. As they say, those were the days.

This one particular day will forever be ingrained in my mind, and even though this event took place over 30 years ago, I am still affected by it. The day started out like any other summer day. It was extremely hot, and being without an air conditioned house left us looking for ways to cool off, so my friends and I would often go to the city pool. There was a group of five or six of us. It was the early 1990's and the rules were much different then. Technology wasn't a thing and cell phones were not around for communication. Kids were out running around with little to no supervision during most of the summer break.

It was a blistering hot summer day and we went swimming for a few hours. When you walked out the door, the air hit you as hard as a 400 degree oven on Thanksgiving. The pavement had heat rays rising as far as you could see. After playing in the cool water, the day ended and we wanted to call for a ride home. We could not use the pool's office phone and were told to go use the payphone across the street, at the restaurant. Again, it was the early '90s and things were different. My sister and a few friends started walking over to the restaurant. We were wearing nothing but our swimsuits and flip flops, with a towel draped over our shoulders. As we walked through the large asphalt parking lot we saw the wonderful A&W sign. Our plan was to call our parents and grab an ice cream float. Only a few of us made it to the restaurant.

    The street that we had to cross was always busy as it led to several businesses. Four lanes, a cross walk and double yellow lines separating them while a caution light hung above. As we started to walk across the street with two car lanes to my left stopped for us, we thought we were safe to go. Unfortunately, in a matter of seconds of crossing, an 80-year-old woman veered over the double yellow lines going an estimated 35 miles per hour (according to the police) and slammed into me. If I hadn't been a tall kid, I most likely would have died. I got hit right below my left hip. Apparently, I pushed my sister ahead of me so she would not get hit, but I don't remember anything about it. I flipped up in the air and landed on my head and back. The lady left the scene and didn't return until she realized that she hit me. To this day, I have no idea what she was thinking or what made her drive away from the scene.

An ambulance came right away and took me up to the hospital where my grandmother was in the emergency room for her shift as an emergency room nurse. I was scared as all can be and my head was the size of a watermelon. Gravel, glass and other road debris were embedded in my back and other exposed areas. The scarring is still noticeable 30+ years later.

How did this event affect my life? I immediately was terrified to cross any street, cars or not. This took a few years where I could take a step into the street without almost having a panic attack. When I started driving, I was nervous about the same situation happening while being a new driver. This was when I was first diagnosed with PTSD by a therapist. Many years later, I still will have images of a car coming out of my peripheral vision darting out at me. This happens less often than when I was younger, but something that I will always be aware of.

A few short years later, I played basketball in the Amateur Athletic Union, a team not affiliated with my school, with a group of kids from other schools. Practices were often held during the summer, and we would travel to tournaments across the state. Looking back, it was probably my greatest time while growing up. Our coach was amazing, but also required all of us to be on time, otherwise playing time would be cut short. I was a starter and did not want to disappoint the coach and further let my team down.

    The summer between my 7th and 8th grade year was filled with basketball practice and workouts. I didn't live far from where we practiced and would often ride my bike because my parents were at work.

    On one of these summer days, my friend had stayed the night and we were both going to practice the next morning. We woke up ready to go to practice early in the morning. It typically took around 10 to 15 minutes to get to the gym where we had practice. The sun was bright, the air was still, and the heat was about to set in. My friend and I ate breakfast and took off on our bikes. Being involved in athletics, we were very competitive and always trying to outdo the other person. In this case, we were trying to get to the gym as fast as we could. Near my house, there were many large hills and streets that were extremely steep. As we rode on top of one of the biggest hills in the area, we geared up and started racing down. As teenagers do, we went as fast as we could, peddling at high speeds. Wind blowing through our hair as if we were driving around a speed boat. I found out later from the police, we were most likely going at minimum 30 miles per hour.

So what happened? Here I was going over an assumed 30 miles per hour down a steep hill with no helmet. Back in the early 1990's they were not mandatory. At the speed I was going, braking immediately was going to be a challenge. My friend was behind me and saw a car pull out of a driveway just a short distance ahead of me. I can't remember much about what happened, but I hit the back of the car and flipped over it. Both the lady whose car I hit and my friend said I flew at least 10 to 15 feet in front of the car, and when I landed, I was inches away from the curb. This could have ended my life, but instead I was left with a major concussion, two shattered big toes and road rash all over my body. The driver completely shook from a scene that could have come out of an action-packed movie. I can't imagine what she must have gone through for years to come due to the loud bang of the bike crinkling the bumper of her car.

During my recovery, I was more upset about missing the rest of basketball and worried I would not be ready to play football in the fall. That summer, I spent six weeks on the couch. Both of my big toes looked like enlarged fully cooked sausage links wrapped in sterile white gauze. Nightmares and glimpses of what happened flashed at a moment's notice. At the time, I had no idea how this was going to affect me as the years passed. From that point on, anything that would dart in front of me would shake me, again. Everything I knew about PTSD from my earlier hit and run was still fresh. Now it was just intensified and would affect me for years to come. To this day I am sometimes leery about things coming from all sides.

My friends, family and others tried to understand what was going on in my head, but I was so young I did not understand everything myself. Adults and kids could see how it affected me physically, but not the deeper impact it had on my mental health. This incident has had major consequences that have resulted in fear throughout my life.

As I've coped with the repercussions of my own trauma, it has helped to hear others' stories. I met Mike Lee while I was applying for a recruiting role where he worked. I didn't get that position, but I respected and wanted to learn from him. During one of our coffee meetings, I asked him to share his recollections of how he grew up and the trauma he had experienced and how that has influenced his experience with hidden disabilities. This is what he shared:

Mike Lee~

The cabin rests quiet and easy, smoke curling lazily from its stone chimney, up to and through and over the still branches of a lazy pine. I can see this cabin, but don't know what it is. My vision is blurry, and everything I see needs cataloging, to be inventoried. An act that itself is foreign to my young mind.

I watch my hand stretch over the cabin, feeling its softness, then the cold metal. I'm not sure what this toothy, metal thing is. But I can see more cabins fade underneath it, underneath the green, not-nearly-so-soft covering that wraps the cabins and the metal thing.

All these years later, this memory persists. I know the location, Camp Lawroweld in the mountains of rural Maine, not far from where I was born. I can do the math around this memory, with the slightly shocking realization that I was probably younger than a year, two at most.

But what I remember most is the deep sense of peace and safety. All was right in the world. I was warm even though the air was chilly. The cabins-in-the-trees sleeping bag was my nest, keeping me warm against the chilly evening, mountain breeze. I was where I belonged. To this day I feel that innocent confidence and bliss.

Somewhere in the 49 years since that chilly evening, life chipped away at that bliss, like the way I pick at the gingerbread house candies. It starts out perfect, or at least beautiful. But time and itchy fingers pull at the beauty, until the bright colors are gone, revealing the fragile sugar glue holding the structure together.

Now as I move through the middle years of middle life, I see how strong the truths are that are formed in early life. And yet those truths tell a different story as life moves on. And I'm only now realizing that it has always been me picking the candies off that gingerbread house. But that's how it's supposed to be, maybe. I'm still figuring this out, but more and more it seems to me that life is all about picking apart that little house and eating its little candies.

I was raised in a conservative, Christian tradition. A tradition that, at least in how I interpreted it, was all about making something of myself to prove my worth to that tradition and its community. Proving who I should be, more than who I am. And that "should be" constantly conflicted with the reality of life's experiences. Those experiences always seemed to fall short, with each day's stories ending a few paragraphs shy of "happily ever after."

I interpreted those experiences as me falling short. Which meant that I must be letting down the people around me with whom I shared that community and tradition.

As a young child, I translated these experiences into a constant striving to belong. Each place I went, I looked around for the rules, the edges, within which I could find safety and belonging. Sometimes I wonder what I would see if I could stand outside myself and watch the old movie reels of those younger years. To see the look in my eyes, my posture, the lilt in my voice as I counted down in a game of "Hide and Seek."

Would I be able to find anyone? Was I picked as the seeker just so everyone could disappear and go play without me? I still remember the anxiety as I opened my eyes from the countdown, wondering if the quiet and lack of any presence of other kids meant my fear was confirmed. These fears were only magnified by bullying as a "teacher's kid" and the child sexual abuse I experienced at the hands of bullies and family.

My childhood became a dark place, with few friends and even fewer places of true belonging. This darkness gave birth to an early sense of always and ever-present anxiety. Anxiety was so present that I'm only coming to realize its constant, low hum, as if it was the soundtrack to my life.

Indeed, anxiety truly was the soundtrack of my life. In high school I opted not to play sports, afraid of locker rooms and what rewards my lack of athletic skill might yield.

My first jobs became my early "out" during high school. I realize now how much of a "stick in the mud" my life became in those early years. Beginning at 15 I held two jobs at any given time, sometimes three. Most of these jobs were solitary, where I could set my own schedule, put my Walkman headphones on and disappear into my own world. All while working hard to earn kudos that, it turns out, were very easy to come by. If I worked hard, I didn't need to think about the friendships I didn't develop and the early collaboration skills I didn't develop until my 40s.

My ability to work hard became a kind of belonging; one where the affirmation I (often) received became an ill-fitting replacement to communal, relational belonging. With every raise and promotion, it simply upped the ante to belong. What I couldn't understand was how each achievement still left me feeling like I was falling short of true acceptance by the people in my life.

This lack of true relationships, combined with a frenetic pursuit of achievement created a new cycle ... a constant push to please the people around me. Combined with the recent, raw, but as-yet-unattended experiences of child abuse, this created a sense of worthlessness and personal unworthiness. Worthlessness and unworthiness told me over and over how much I didn't belong in my community or relationships. And of course, this just fed the cycle of striving to achieve, please people and inevitable worthlessness.

Early adulthood was mildly, but deceptively, better. The ability to create my own life and pick my own relationships meant I could more easily opt out of true relational depth. And yet I began to see the mirage I had created in my life.

What I didn't realize at the time, was that the relational depth I opted out of was creating a contrast I could see more clearly with each passing life phase. While my broken relational mechanisms and habits kept true depth at arms length, I could see with greater clarity what I wanted: trust, belonging, and transformation.

~Mike Lee

Childhood trauma has made my life as an adult difficult at times. There are times when an event will happen, and I will get extremely angry. I get taken back to the place where I was when the trauma occurred. Now in my 40's, I am trying to recognize that the events are in my past. Those events have followed me around like a dark shadow. Childhood trauma can make anyone, even a war veteran, want to shrink inside a small crater.

Silence Could Kill

Oh, the teenage years. This is when you can start to hear and see where many issues from early childhood start to affect people with hormones and puberty coming into play. Any trauma that has not been treated prior to this, or at least recognized, can rear its ugly head during this period.

Teenagers by nature are still learning the processes through which they become adults. They make impulse decisions based on what they feel, not always what they actually need or want. As adults, we have to acknowledge how teenagers cope with trauma and that every teenager's problems are not the same. Today, while writing this book, I have two teenagers who have issues of their own. I am aware that I simply never truly know how they are feeling on the inside just by seeing their outside appearance. Many teenagers have not yet been taught or equipped to handle outside pressures that affect their hidden disabilities. This isn't their fault. Teenagers often feel they are alone and adults can't understand what they are going through.

What happens when the problems that they are facing internally are not solved or addressed? They stay inside and fester until the person either takes action, or worst-case scenario, commits suicide. Suicide is a significant problem with our teenage population. According to America's Health Ratings, 14 out of 100,000 of teenagers commit suicide. Let's put that in real time perspective. In Los Angeles, CA, the population for teenagers from 11-17 in 2021 was 890,466. With those numbers, in 2021, it would be as if over 63,000 teenagers committed suicide. Let's break down those numbers for a city much smaller. In 2021, the teen population (ages 10-17) of Reno, NV was 22,475. This indicates that, with these statistics, roughly over 300 teenagers could have committed suicide in the city of Reno in 2021. I don't need to be an expert in psychology or anything else to know that this is alarming and we need as a society to get this under control.

Suicide: soo-uh-sahd

noun

The act or an instance of taking one's own life voluntarily and intentionally

In 1999, I almost took my life. I was 16 years old and the people around me had no idea how depressed and filled with fear I was. I was often confused and anything that anyone said could trigger me into a deep dark place. I had a car and often thought about driving towards oncoming traffic.

I played off my emotions and hid from the world. The night I almost took my life, I can remember feeling so low, so saddened that nothing seemed to matter anymore. I was skipping school, drinking, smoking marijuana, and at times hanging out with crowds that I probably should have avoided. What was I doing or thinking? I wasn't. I didn't have the tools nor the confidence to face the fears that I was experiencing. Partially, I had no idea and therefore couldn't communicate the feelings I was feeling. As I sat on my bed one cold winter evening, I held a Remington .22 caliber revolver, with my finger on the trigger. At that moment at 16, I was terrified, and it felt like a large black hole to come out of.

    Now, in my 40's, I cannot remember anything about why I wanted to pull the trigger that night. All I know is that I was extremely low and nothing seemed to matter. Fortunately for me, my mother suspected something was up and intervened. If she hadn't, I don't know that I would be here today. That night was difficult. I had a choir concert and had to get ready for that after everything that was going on. Looking back on that evening, I should have just stayed home. I was a mess. My world had crashed down and I had no idea why. Here I was, playing varsity football and baseball and appeared to be on the highest mountain you can achieve. How was anyone supposed to see that I was in such a dark place?

In the coming months, I would start therapy and have my first diagnosis of clinical depression. At the time I had no idea what it was, and really didn't care. On the surface, I was a 16-year-old kid. I loved playing sports, lifting weights and hanging out with my buddies. The problem was that I was avoiding everything that was bringing me down. My grades were awful and I couldn't ever understand the subjects. My parents were always stressed about work. It was as if I was too busy to understand what I was really thinking or doing. Survival was all I was trying to navigate, yet I only realize this now twenty-five years later. I never wanted to be home alone and spent as much time as I could at my best friends or girlfriend's house. Oftentimes I would stay away from home for multiple days and on weekends.

That spring marked the biggest fight my dad and I ever had. Again, there is a common theme here. I can't remember what the fight was about. Whatever it was, it made my dad so mad that he pushed me onto the couch and raised his fist like he was going to hit me. Towering over me like a grizzly over its prey, I lay there helpless to what could happen. His arms were so big that we often joked he had inserted softballs into his biceps. As I said earlier, his abuse of me had always been verbal. My dad never came close to hitting me until that day. In this case, instead of freeze, I waited until I felt it was safe. I remember getting off the couch and running outside. I had never run so fast out of my own house in my life. Now, not only was I afraid of the voice coming at me, but I was also afraid of the physical punishment that seemed to be coming. Outside there were no smells and my natural feeling was to get as far away as I could. In my hands, I held the keys to my car and the house. My adrenaline at an all time high and muscles tense. Standing on the cement porch, hovering over the black railings in a fury, he screamed to give him my keys. I did, in the form of throwing them like a fastball right at him. I can still remember my arm throwing them. The keys moist with my sweaty hand, yet still cold and jagged was the only thing I had on me. The sound of the keys hitting his chest was like a thud of an arrow piercing a target. At that point I had no idea what to do, but I knew I couldn't be around my dad.

    The relationship that I had with my father was only decent at best. He was stubborn, but so was I–after all, what 16-year-old isn't? The problem was that neither of us had any awareness of what the other was going through. When my father was a kid, discipline was very different than it was when I was a kid. My grandfather was a severe alcoholic and I heard stories of his anger. But I was fighting inner demons and my dad had no clue that was going on either. We could barely talk to each other and the only time that we truly got along was when we were out in the woods driving around looking for animals. For years my father and I would butt heads and challenge each other like we were two rams fighting for dominance. It wasn't until recently that we've truly begun communicating. Although things are much better now, the damage that was done has haunted me as I've raised my own children and has affected many parts of my life.

Clinical Depression
Noun:
a depression so severe as to be considered abnormal, either because of no obvious environmental causes, or because the reaction to unfortunate life circumstances is more intense or prolonged than would generally be expected.

I would love to say that this experience was the only time that I have ever had suicidal thoughts, but honestly, I can't remember a decade where I haven't struggled with the thought, although never have I acted or made an attempt since that night when I was 16 years old. I can say that I was one of the lucky ones I guess, but I was about to buckle up for one of the most challenging decades of my young life, that included a divorce, more abuse, military trauma, having two kids while being stranded 3,000 miles from friends or family, and being a college drop-out for the second time with one quarter to graduate.

I am currently in the process of switching careers from being a technical recruiter to teaching. I am substitute teaching and loving most of it. I worked at a juvenile detention home. Working with a variety of people at all levels from our youth to our adults, my experience covers generations from the Baby Boomers to Gen Z. You want to know what I have noticed in EVERY people related job that I have had? All people want is for someone to listen. This applies 100% more with our youth. Don't judge them all by the cover that they wear. Truly, if you haven't walked in their shoes, listen and learn. Imagine what would happen if every adult reached out to a kid who may be the "troubled kid" or the "weird kid". How about the kids who you think are thriving? You can't be sure with anyone based on what you see. Millions of lives could be changed and how many suicides would we prevent? Just reaching out and speaking to our youth could change their life. Feeling heard and not alone would greatly help this situation.

When looking into how I wanted this book to be written, I wanted to collaborate with others who had experienced similar trauma. I sent a message out to my

LinkedIn network and asked who would be interested in contributing. I had an overwhelming response and one of my connections, a fellow veteran, Lucas Velmer, jumped at the opportunity to share his story.

Lucas Velmer~

When we moved out from my dad's, we moved into a small apartment with my stepdad. My stepdad drank a lot. He did and sold drugs. He was verbally and emotionally abusive to us, and he was physically abusive to my mom.

This had a profound impact on me. Writing about it forces me to remember and visualize things that make me emotional. Even as I write this, I've got to fight back tears. The events from 14 until I left at 18 1/2 changed me forever. I went from being a naïve, outgoing kid, to a dark, depressed teenager seemingly overnight. I couldn't get the validation I needed in myself because I was always berated for doing something wrong, no matter what I did, nothing was good enough. So, I sought validation in others, especially girls because I was more comfortable with them. But this also led to me manipulating them into thinking they were in the wrong regardless of who was responsible. Additionally, as part of my validation complex, I would seek out the girls who appeared to "need help" as if I was going to be their knight and save the day. This led to me helping them with emotional issues, but it also created a tax on me because I would internalize their emotions and almost make them my own as a way to empathize and provide advice. It meant I wouldn't deal with my own emotions, and because I couldn't express my emotions anywhere, I would take it out on them or just shut them out completely. Regardless, I look back at my teenage years in absolute horror because I was a terrible person. I was grief-stricken, guilt-ridden, depressed, and in such pain that any little thing that went wrong pushed me closer and closer to suicide. I just wanted it all to go away. I just wanted the pain to end. In those four years, I cut myself multiple times, I stabbed myself on purpose. The only outlet I had was music and so I buried myself in my room and taught myself how to play the guitar. This is probably the only positive thing to come from those 4 years.

    Coincidentally, it was my stepdad who got me into the guitar. He was a drummer. Despite losing his right hand while working in a sawmill many years prior, he still managed to play and play well. So, I was exposed to music and other musicians which helped me look forward to those rare occasions where all was right with the world.

~Lucas Velmer

As an adult, I look back to those teenage years and can recognize what was going on. Unfortunately, I have had to deal with these behaviors as an adult. As much as I want to say that I didn't do the same things to my own kids. I can't. When my oldest children were born, I was in my early 20's. I didn't know how to discipline correctly. I was angry at my children when they had no reason to be at fault. I was harsh on them and years later learned that the things I was doing were totally abusive. My worst nightmare. As time has gone on, I have learned better techniques to deal with discipline. When my oldest kids were six and eight, I met Meredith who helped me figure out ways to be a better father.

Now, with two more children, I have raised them much differently. Know better, do better. They don't know what getting yelled at is. I don't take out my bad day on them. Not saying that I am a perfect parent by any means. Over the last decade, I have worked hard on leaving things behind, letting go of control and calmly speaking to my children when they do something that they are not supposed to.

War Guilt

Now, before all of you get your underwear in a bunch, I love this country, and anyone will tell you that. With that said, much about this country needs to change and the military branches should be held responsible for change as well. I will be the first to say that I fully understand why we were instructed and taught the way we were. We had to be prepared for war and a few months after I joined, that's where I went.

It was 2001 and I had just graduated high school and thought the world was going to welcome me with open arms and things were just going to happen. Those thoughts quickly vanished three days after I moved to Eugene, OR for college. To my dismay, my car got broken into right in front of my apartment. Life check: I was in the real world and not with little old town folk anymore. In a mere six months time, I headed back to that town to figure life out, or so I thought.

Uncle Sam is always hiring, so I talked to both of my grandparents and a few others who had served in the military to get their opinions. After some thought and inflated expectations thanks to my recruiter, I signed the next five years of my life away to the Navy. My experience overall with

44

the military was fine. I am not going to sit here and tell you that I loved it and I would do it all over if I had the chance. I wouldn't. The reality is that I had zero intent of joining the military until I had very few choices in front of me. I didn't have the maturity to handle college at that age. I never learned the tools needed to be successful and I never owned that I struggled as a student. I did what I had to keep playing sports and avoid negative attention from my parents. So, one could say I was lazy. Alternatively, one could say that I struggled so much with actually being home that I was not ever mentally stable enough to grasp basic studying skills.

    My idea of what that first night in the military would be like is something that I–and most veterans–will never forget. Imagine taking an old city bus packed full, with boys, not quite men, just realizing what they truly have signed up for and what was waiting for us after the long ride from Chicago O'Hare Airport. It was at that very moment that I realized I was in the wrong place. I wanted to go home. It's one thing for the recruiter and veterans to tell you what you are going to experience, but then it hits you. Prior to this moment, you at least had some rights. The world had rules that people had to follow, otherwise there would be consequences. Now, I am not saying that the military doesn't have rules and regulations. The Uniform Code of Military

Justice (USMJ) governs the military branches. The standard laws are still in place, but this code is added to any military member. The rules are just more strict and are only followed when issues are brought up. Guess how many internal issues are brought up? Typically, the only time people got into trouble was when they got into trouble outside of the base.

    The night that I arrived at Naval Station Great Lakes, where Navy boot camp was located, I ran around like a chicken with my head cut off. Imagine an ant farm, but with stations where they stop to get yelled at by the queen. This was the first night of terror. I was also terrified because prior to the trip, I had been smoking marijuana and had taken mushrooms only a couple of weeks prior. Not the smartest thing to do, but I clearly wasn't thinking. In fact, I think I was subconsciously wanting to fail the urinalysis. Soon I would find out that if I had failed the test, I would have just been sent to the barracks and waited 30 days until I was clean. Damn.

    We were taken to a huge warehouse with tables 20 feet long, lined up with blue sweats with the words Navy on them in gold writing, black tactical flight boots, dark blue pants (known as dungarees), blue collared shirts, Navy blue coveralls and every size and color of uniform from work to dress. In the midst of trying to stuff each article of clothing into a sea bag, you were sent to the urinals to do your urine test. My hands were sweaty, I was exhausted, and could barely hold the little plastic cup I was supposed to use. I stood there in distress trying to go pee. After several minutes, I dropped the cup and all of the urine that I was able to get was now in the toilet. Tears would have fallen from my face, but I was too distraught with fear they wouldn't come. What came next? My first experience being yelled at and made to feel extremely small. How did I respond? I responded the way that I knew how. I stayed quiet and out of the way, as I had learned to do while growing up.

Each branch of the military has its own flaws and the system has to grow and change. The soldiers, airmen, sailors and marines live a life where they are told to do something and they do it. In the military, you are not allowed to question authority. You don't question your orders. Bootcamp in many ways is the beginning of turning someone hard, and transforming them into a rule-obeying machine. Ask why you have to do something? The answer you will get is that "it's above your paygrade/rank."

In my own experiences as a civilian, I have not ever had to go through that again. I do understand that the majority of the civilian sector of the United States does not have to worry about imminent global threats and they do not have to go through the training to handle those situations. The thought of having to do things the way they are just because we have always done them, doesn't sit right. Do we really need to turn our young military members into robots that perform without questions or checks and balances? I don't pretend to have the answers. What do we have? Experience with all of the mental anguish that comes along from a system that should be reworked.

Psychology and the way that we try to train folks in high-stress situations can be modified. We don't fight wars like we used to, so why do we have to train like we used to? Now, this is speaking to the general military member professional, and does not represent the special forces. Those folks have a different life and I don't pretend to be in that group nor have had any special forces training. With that said, I don't have to be an expert to see the rates of suicide affecting veterans.

There are multiple organizations that are trying to help this issue. According to the Veterans Administration, 22 veterans a day commit suicide. Along with that devastating number, veterans are 1.5 times more likely to commit suicide than those peers who are still active in the military. Let that sink in. They were all dealing with hidden issues that ended up being too much for them to take on. Many stay silent for fear of society putting a label on them as *"One of those PTSD vets."*

After the ending of World War II, a shift happened in the United States and the perception of veterans. We call that era of veterans the Greatest Generation. People knew why we were at war. There seemed to be a purpose. When those folks came home after serving, they were heroes. Veterans of the Korean War, Vietnam, Desert Storm, and most recently, Iraq/Afghanistan have not been treated the same way. Videos and pictures of veterans coming back from Vietnam should bring a tear to your eye and a cringe in your heart. These folks were drafted to go to a war and had no idea what they were getting into. And when they came home they were spit on, protested against and called "baby killers" and a wrath of other things. I can only imagine the mental issues that those veterans have faced since they arrived home. This can be seen after other wars as well. Many civilians don't think about it or choose to ignore what happens to a veteran after they have served their country. We were told that while we were traveling, we had to travel in our formal uniforms. When I was on the plane, I tried to make myself as small as possible. People were either all for the Iraq War or completely against it. At the time, I thought we were doing what we needed to do to keep that country safe. Years later I have come to the opinion, we shouldn't have been there at all.

I am one of the "lucky" ones. I have always had a tremendous level of support dealing with many of the mental and physical disabilities that I have. Was the military the cause of all of them? No, but five years working on an aircraft carrier flight deck will age your body quickly. A good portion of veterans have a disability that is tied to military service. Applicable diagnosed disabilities can be found through the Veterans Administration's website. According to the VA Claims insider, in 2023, the fourth highest claim for veterans is Post Traumatic Stress Disorder (PTSD). Can you see this disability? How about Tinnitus or Migraines from a Traumatic Brain Injury (TBI)? Are you able to recognize these by just being near someone? The answer is fairly simple. You can't.

Tinnitus tin-ni-tus

noun:

ringing or buzzing in the ears

Migraine mi-graine

Noun:

A recurrent throbbing headache that typically affects one side of the head and is often accompanied by nausea and disturbed vision.

As explained by author Herb Tompson, former Green Beret: "Here's a myth, veterans kill themselves because of the horrors of war. They sit there thinking about combat and the ugliness they experienced. Everyone I know who chose or attempted suicide ended it because of a loss of belonging, relationship turmoil, past trauma, financial hardship, etc. High stress events in anyone's life. Veterans were trained that killing is a solution to a problem. Maybe that continues as they confront their demons."

Herb is not the only one who has these thoughts and opinions about the topic. Veterans go through hell and when they think that the DD214 releases them from battle, they are devastated to find out this is when the real work begins. A DD214 is the final letter that you receive as you exit the military and become a civilian. It acts as your proof of service and holds all of your military dates and awards. As veterans, we are told that we are going to be taken care of in return for volunteering for this country. The truth is that we were misled. I have heard over and over again from hundreds of veterans over the last 16 years how hard it is to get help from the VA. Most of the time they will quit trying to get help and that is when the real suffering begins.

People, as a general rule, don't like ugly, but sometimes it takes ugly for people to want things to change. From 2018 to 2019, over 20 veterans committed suicide *on the grounds of the Veterans Administration*. Those numbers continue to soar as the 20-year-anniversary of Iraqi Freedom veterans experience relapsed trauma. One of the most notable cases in the last few years was highly publicized. Reported by Military Times, Marine Col. Jim Turner put on his uniform and drove to the front of the VA facility and shot himself. He left a strong message on a note next to his body where he lay covered in blood. The note read, "I bet if you look at the 22 suicides a day you will see VA screwed up in 90 percent."

Veterans struggle with mental health and often have no idea how to get out of their own way. We are told very early on in the military that "you don't go to medical." You don't see a doctor (well, no one actually *tells* you not to go to medical, but it is heavily looked down upon.). If you are hurt or injured, you are a liability and cannot perform at the highest level.

Personally, the fear and struggle for me came a few short years after I got out of the service. What caused me such grief? I wasn't boots on the ground with an M-16 rifle knocking down walls and doors in Iraq. I was on the USS Kitty Hawk launching war machines to destroy certain targets. Now, I am living with tremendous guilt about what I was part of.

War isn't pretty. War isn't a video game. War isn't medals and honor. War is a situation where lives are destroyed, and lives are dismantled. Mental anguish as well as physical anguish follows those involved in war, on both sides of the fight. What I have gone through mentally, post-military, is far worse than when I was in the military.

Post-military trauma is what gets in the way of healing for a long time for many veterans, and some don't ever recover or learn to cope. There are things that I feel and go through that not even my kids or wife truly understand. We all have issues, some more severe than others, but issues nonetheless. All things considered, many veterans are afraid to admit or don't want the follow up questions to why they are the way they are.

What keeps me up at night and is part of my post military trauma? Okay, here we go. My job in the United States Navy was launching aircraft off of the flightdeck on the USS Kitty Hawk (CV-63) aircraft carrier. I loved my job, mostly.

53

We were up late working outside with our hands. We were the "blue collar" workers of the ship. Dirty, greasy and full of piss and vinegar. As an Aviation Boatswain's Mate (Equipment) the expectation when we were out to sea was that we would work 18-hour shifts on normal days. Like most military branches, hours don't mean much. More or less, it is a shift without a clock in/clock out situation. It was what it was. Sailors were extremely tired, and many were only 18 years old. The responsibility of launching million-dollar aircraft was left in the hands of young men and women who were physically and emotionally drained. One could say that we were zombies surviving on adrenaline and recycled coffee. During our deployment to Iraq, we had over 80 aircraft onboard. A standard FA-18E Super Hornet during training missions would weigh in from anywhere to around 25,000 lbs. up to 35,000 lbs. Now, here is where this starts to make you think, and what still haunts me. Each aircraft would leave the flight deck weighing close to 100,000 lbs. depending on the mission they were on. When they came back onto the carrier, they would weigh in at less than 20,000 lbs. Fuel tanks, missiles, rockets and everything that could be dropped, was dropped. Fear and destruction were going on and we were causing it.

The reality of war is ultimately death and destruction. I was part of causing the loss of thousands of lives. Can I be positive that there were Iraqi civilians that were not killed during these missions? No. I have no idea, but I do know that I had a part in the loss of those thousands of lives. My entire mission was to launch war machines into the air knowing where and what they were going to do. When coming back from the missions, each aircraft would paste stickers up near the call sign of the pilot of the ammunition that they dropped. As a sailor at the time, I thought that it was cool as hell. Now, it haunts me. My PTSD isn't traditional, my onset came after I was out of the service for a few years.

Imagine sitting on a commuter train in Japan, coming back from Iraq with your buddies and saying, "Who drops bombs . . . we drop bombs." Now I think, why in the hell would anyone think that was okay? We did and I am not proud of that moment. I can only imagine what the elders and the people of Japan thought of what we were saying. Talk about a naive young man who was manipulated into thinking what we did was right. At the time, we had no idea what was really going on, and, really, to this day, not many of us veterans know. We just have to live with what we did and accept that somewhere along the line, leaders of this country failed us.

The mental issues that come along with thinking about that can be deafening. There were nights where I would have severe nightmares and see blurred images of people I never knew. I would often think about the destruction I was part of but I chose to suppress my emotions for a long time. After many years and a few life situations, I found myself again contemplating suicide. Obviously, I am writing this today so I didn't pursue those thoughts, but they were there. I made the decision to go to therapy after. I can't believe that it took me that long to make that decision.

In the end, I have found comfort in knowing that I am not alone with my struggles regarding my military experience. The number of veterans out there who still struggle and do not have the support is horrible. We are not able to rely on the Veterans Administration or government to truly take care of veterans, so we as a nation have to do a better job of it. How can we act on this for change? Simple. Reach out to your veteran organizations and see where you can volunteer. Veteran support is something that we all need. Don't put us in a box where we can fester over what we have gone through and done. Oftentimes, veterans just want to be heard without judgment. We don't want sympathy, but we could use some empathy. Remember that the veterans who served did not make the choice to do what they did, they were told to do it.

They were given orders to carry out and were following those orders.

Lucas Velmer~

I went to basic training in July of 2000. I struggled at reception for about a week; I ended up in the hospital due to dehydration and anxiety attacks. Then I woke up one day and I was fine. I got picked up at reception to go to my BCT company and was met with something I had never experienced in my life. But I was great at compartmentalizing and adapting. Even when I called my girlfriend on Sunday morning, three weeks into basic, and she told me she was seeing someone else, I just shut off my emotions and let it slow drip throughout. Compartmentalize and adapt. That's exactly what I did. So much so that my drill sergeants didn't even know my name until graduation day.

The whole reason we were called down to BIAP was to divert traffic and prevent unauthorized access around voting centers. Our mission was to help traffic flow through checkpoints to support the push for voting and a democratic election. The mission had us hauling barriers and equipment on large trucks on all sorts of roads, trails, and through neighborhoods. You name it, we were there making more enemies than friends, working at all hours and tearing down *power lines and everything else. We got attacked by small arms fire and attempted IED detonations multiple times. To this day, I have to actively remind myself that trash, potholes, and anything else on the road is not an attempt on my life.*

    That particular deployment was tough and events from that deployment are the source of my PTSD (along with other health problems), which would only get further exacerbated on subsequent deployments. SCUD alerts in the middle of the night. Patriot missiles firing off within 50 feet of our tent. Gas mask drills all the time. Even when I returned, every time I heard my alarm go off, I would scramble to find my mask. It lasted for months. We started in Kuwait and made our way up to An Najif in MOPP4. That had to be the longest drive ever...miles long convoy driving 25-30 mph. Anyways, Najif is where we spent most of our time there digging in the division HQ areas. After Najif was cleared, we went up to just south of Baghdad. The most significant mission there was when we were called to haul away abandoned BMPs that were fully loaded. We had to unload all of the munitions with the EOD guy, who then blew them in place in a safe area nearby. While we were there, the locals would come and ask us why the people with tanks shot everything that moved. People, livestock, everything. Our SITREP was kicked back because it included what we were told by the locals. All we could tell them was to visit their district center to hopefully get reimbursed for their losses. Not long after this mission, we had to resupply on the other side of Baghdad in Balad. The lead vehicle missed a turn and put us with our tractor-trailers in a traffic jam in a traffic circle. I, along with several others, had to get out and try to direct traffic at least enough for us to get through. I got hit and almost ran over. We got attacked there, just sitting ducks, people running and screaming everywhere with gunshots and grenades going off. It was mass chaos. To this day, I still struggle in crowds because of this. We did end up making it with only minor damage to vehicles. This resupply would be our last in this area because we had to move again. This time all the way to Mosul.

~Lucas Velmer

Fred has become a friend of mine over the last few years. Our paths crossed professionally, after we were both out of the military. He was working in a remarkable company helping veterans find employment. The company unfortunately closed, but Fred and I have retained a friendship on a personal and professional level. I am excited he gets to share his story and reach anyone who wants to hear it.

Fred Melvin~

My military career was full of contradictions and painful lessons. I am immensely grateful at this point in my life for all of it; it made me who I am and was meaningful work that challenged me. I enlisted in the U.S. Army at Fort Meade, Maryland, in June 2002, at the age of 17. After several run-ins with the military police and other police, getting in trouble on and off base, I thought it would be funny to go be one of them. There was not much thought in picking my job past that; I lacked prospects and confidence, wanted money for school, and wanted to see the world. Later, I found out that the traditional law enforcement I saw on the base where I lived was just one function of the job, one you only normally did when in garrison and always competing with lots of combat training. Several times during my training, I heard, "The MP stands for Multi-Purpose." I did not truly understand this until after reporting to my initial duty station in Wiesbaden, Germany, in a Divisional Military Police Company.

When I got off the plane in Frankfurt, I should have known I was headed for a rough time when the MP at the airport took one look at my orders and said sarcastically, "Divisional MP Company? Have fun with that!" We worked long hours and got a few days off. I learned a widely adopted tactic for not getting called in to cover for someone on "road duty" was to start drinking as early as possible on your day off. I arrived around November, and after a grueling law enforcement and combat training schedule, by March of 2003, I was in Iraq. I was just 18 years old. 1st Armored Division spent 16 months in theater; we were the first major unit in decades to go past a 12-month combat tour, and after us, it became the norm. There was no real mission that we understood at ground level; everything was on fire and disorganized, and our company got dispersed all over the theater, performing widely different missions in support of the Tank Division. I remember the dehumanizing culture when talking about the enemy and many of us being in moral conflict with the entire war.

    Our little platoon ended up doing route clearance in Al Anbar province out of LSA Dogwood for the first five months. We would get one or two days off a month, 12 hours on, 12 hours off, driving up and down the road looking for roadside bombs, blowing them up with a squad of unhinged Alabama National Guard Engineers. We found one almost every week, sometimes several a day. This was not what I thought I was signing up for when I joined. There was so much stress; we got shot at by our own troops, mainly Marines; there were times we were only saved by the incompetence of the enemy; and it felt like any day could be the day one of the bombs did what it was designed to do. I became nihilistic, lost faith a bit in the *meaning of it all, and changed my dog tags from Episcopalian to atheist. I remember going to visit my parents in the winter of 2003 and considering not coming back. My mother took a picture, which she still shows me when we talk about the time. In the picture, I look unrecognizable, gaunt, dead in the eyes, and devoid of joy. I found it hard to find anything exciting.*

This experience set me on a path of drinking and adrenaline-seeking; it was normal in my unit to take risks. I remember a place in Wiesbaden we called "church." Europalace was a dance club open until morning, where we drank heavily daily (religiously), sometimes only returning in time to change and stumble to morning formation. This was not just for the junior guys; our leaders did this too. I remember when we deployed, several people initially had alcohol withdrawal symptoms. We joked about having the shakes. When we got back from Iraq after 16 months, it was a nonstop party; everyone was drunk, and for a 19-year-old kid who felt lost and used, I was finding it a great escape. I hung out with German punk rock kids and traveled; I had fun, but I was learning how to be a completely different person at work, at home, and at play. I was losing myself in the process of compartmentalizing. Things became normal to me, like drinking and driving, drugs, divorce, and driving fast.

When I got stationed in Oklahoma, I was not yet 20 years old. I became a sergeant, got into the local punk rock scene, and went to Military Police Investigator School. It was a strange double life. When off duty, I was using a fake ID, going to punk rock shows and parties, and drinking heavily. When on duty, I was investigating a wide range of crimes, many involving alcohol, and even doing underage drinking sting operations at local bars. It was exciting; I enjoyed the contradiction of carrying such authority at work, wearing plain clothes with a concealed weapon, and being a wild man off work. This was not unique to me—this off-duty culture of blowing off steam. Many of my leaders celebrated drinking alcohol, and many openly cheated on their partners, especially when we were not home and training somewhere.

Fast forward several units, another deployment, and promotion all the way to Sergeant First Class (E-7), I became pretty good at balancing my thrill-seeking, my family life, and my serious Military Police senior NCO business. At my unit at Fort Lewis, Washington, I was a platoon sergeant, and by many measures, I was excelling at my craft. I had earned my master's degree, owned two houses, had a loving wife, was a father to two amazing boys, and was very good at being who the Army needed me to be at work.

One day in formation, I heard my First Sergeant say something to us that I felt was a bit absurd at the time. He said, "Your professional life should mirror your personal life," meaning if who you are at work is who you are at home, you can be honest in the way you live, and these things don't come in conflict with one another. Looking back at this statement, this was a great piece of wisdom and something I could not hear through my filter of ego and alcoholism. After all, he did not really know me; how could he?

It's funny how much one night can completely change your life. Looking back, all the warnings were there if I was in a position to pay attention to them. Not long after my First Sergeant gave that advice, I was at a punk show in downtown Olympia and drank some shots of tequila and whiskey with my brother. I had also fallen several times on the beer-soaked dance floor during the show and was a bit of a mess. When it was time to go, someone asked me if I was sure I could drive home, and my brother assured this concerned acquaintance that I was a pro at it, on account of my bragging about how many times I had gotten away with it, sometimes with him in the car and by virtue of my being a police officer.

I pulled out on the main street, and seconds later I was pulled over by a state trooper. I told him I was Military Police as it had helped in the past, but he had none of it, and I was arrested. I then had the difficult choice to tell my unit, which I ultimately did, mainly because I knew it would come out when I got my top-secret security clearance renewed. First though, I got a lawyer who helped defer prosecution on the condition I admitted to being an alcoholic, went into an intensive outpatient treatment program, and stayed out of trouble for five years. I was forced into treatment where I heard repeatedly, "You're only as sick as your secrets," so I began to tell mine after hearing some similar ones in my court-mandated AA and outpatient treatment. I told my truths a bit recklessly at first, and it was painful for many people involved. Some of these were secrets I kept from my wife about my behavior with other women, behavior that she was not able to forgive, and we ultimately divorced. I threw myself at the mercy of the military justice system as well, informing that same First Sergeant, who had given me such poignant life advice, about how I had gotten in trouble and what I was doing to rehabilitate. In the end, they took some pity on me because I was a high performer and was seeking help. I still got a poor evaluation report, however, and that would catch up with me.

  Some time passed, and in December 2015, I got caught up with thousands of other senior Noncommissioned Officers who also had blemishes on their records in what was called the

Qualitative Management Process, a downsizing measure that year. I appealed with many character references, but it did no good. I was honorably discharged less than a year later, after 14 years of service. I felt dejected, thrown away, and like I had been betrayed after giving so much to the military. Looking back, it was one of the best things that could have happened. Someone needed to apply the brakes, and I certainly was not going to do it.

    I fell into recruiting when I got out, using investigative skills, interviewing skills, and many other skills I learned in the military. Through this work of helping others and with a home life that allows me to be at home, I have found a cathartic balance, able to be in balance with my personal and professional life for the first time. Since the end of my military career in 2016, I have married an amazing woman who brings out the best in me. I have been alcohol-free for seven years, repaired many relationships, and enjoyed great personal and professional success. I credit a large part of this to my experimenting with psychedelics. After a "bad trip" about a year into my sobriety, I was able to let go of so much that was ego-driven, experiencing what many call an "ego death.". It was closely akin to what others who have been clinically dead for a short time and get resuscitated describe as a feeling of unity and oneness with all things, a loss of self, a bright white light, a feeling of rebirth. It was one of the most profound experiences of my life. Since then, I cry and feel things that I never could before; I don't hold resentments any longer; I have no enemies; I feel at peace more than I don't; it feels unnatural to not tell the truth; and I don't feel the need to seek thrills. I try to stay aware of the interconnectedness of all things and put love and honesty into all I do.

I am grateful for the military; I learned and got exposed to the world. I now enjoy a wonderful life helping others find employment. After having consulted with thousands of veterans on their careers through my work, I find that for many of us, the imbalance between personal life and professional life has long been a struggle that existed throughout our time in the military. I am grateful to be off the military roller coaster of always getting ready to go somewhere, going somewhere, or coming back from somewhere. Always thinking of the future conquest and goal and not being mindful or present. The military taught me a great many things, but it did not teach me compassion or empathy, or how precious our time is on this earth and how connected we all are. I learned that when everything I thought I knew fell apart.

~**Fred Melvin**

This next story holds dear to my heart. ABE3 Tom, who wanted to be anonymous, was a great friend of mine who I served with. He and I grew up together from the rank of senior airman on up. Good times, bad times and everything we experienced, we were together. I love this man, I call brother. Here is his mental health struggle.

Petty Officer 3rd class Tom~

I want to elaborate a little. There were a few moments where the only way to make myself feel better was to hurt myself. I always would carry a pen and would stab myself with it because the pain took my mind off the despair and anger I felt inside. Other times I would punch the locker until my knuckles bleed and drink my own blood. I did this until maybe 2003 when I broke my hand. I had a nervous breakdown where I attacked a few shipmates, Chief had to have a conversation with me. After that conversation I usually tried to talk to myself. I still talk to myself to this day but try to keep that voice down because it calls me awful names that I would rather not say aloud.

I was punching and stabbing myself up until late 2023. I have been out of the military since 2007. The intention was never to break skin, but to cause pain. The pain calmed me down when I had psychotic episodes. At times I had explosive episodes at work and was fired often due to behavioral issues. My low self-esteem to this day and erratic moods have made civilian life extremely difficult. Just recently, I was prescribed a stronger dose of antipsychotic quetiapine.

  The Navy did empower me to work on really expensive equipment, but it was there where I started having psychotic episodes and uncontrollable anger outbursts. Prior to the Navy, I was a caregiver for my little sister and was coined Mr. Mom. I went into the military and came out a full blown alcoholic and drug addict. Up until September of 2023, this year I was an addict. At times I wish I could cry like I used to on deployment. Those cries released so much pain and helped me release everything I was feeling without the use of drugs or alcohol. These days I feel very numb or angry most of the time. When I get angry I obsess about these things that anger me. Overtime, I have become a shell of a human.

  I am on multiple psychotic drugs to help my hidden disabilities. Currently, I don't have a driver's license because of the medications that I am taking. Because of the danger of my medications and side effects, I am not safe to drive. Additionally, I have learned to stay away from a few medications that were more harmful than good in my opinion. I am on Abilify and Lurasidone. At times I wanted to rip the skin off my bones. Another one that I have taken and have to avoid is Akathisia. For me, this is the worst side effect of any mental health medications you can have. I literally twisted the skin on my chest and arms trying to calm myself down to stop moving. It's how Parkinson's disease feels like I have been told. It is the worst feeling ever. I can't sit still. These drugs are no joke because they may be initially effective, but they turn on you and, bam, you get these crazy side effects in my experience. These are some of the side effects of the treatments or when I had serotonin syndrome for five years. They were giving me antidepressants. It wasn't until a couple of years ago the psychologist realized that I was experiencing psychosis and SSR. This caused my manic episodes to be worse. It was like adding fuel to the fire. Even with a diagnosis, people can wait many years before finding the right medications. When I could not sit still and had unwanted movements, I honestly thought about drowning myself in the bathtub. People have described it as literally not knowing what to do with yourself. The worst side effect felt like wanting to rip my skin off my body. It's a terrible feeling you can't explain unless you experience it. This is what it's like living with these disabilities.

    Detoxing from antipsychotic medications has been said to be worse than detoxing from heroin. Many people will have horrible migraines for months.

During a few deployments out to sea, I thought about committing suicide while on steam watch. This was a task that involved different stations of the catapult. A few stations were located on the catwalk on the flight deck. This is the platform right below where the aircraft are launched. In the middle of the night I stared at the dark sea and wanted to end it all. The feeling of abandonment by my family, made Navy life much more difficult. At times I hit my head with the flashlight and cried for like thirty minutes. This was the first time I think I hurt myself as a relief for stress.

Among these things, I also have sleep apnea which makes a lot of treatments complicated. I just remembered that I am addicted to anger and pain as a maladaptive coping mechanism just like drugs and alcohol. The pain is very addictive, for me. I also would burn my hands with my lighters to release my pain. It was a maladaptive mechanism. My psychiatrist told me to use a rubber band instead but the pain was not strong enough. The prescription Gabapentin helped me with that a little.

To add to all of the other issues, I also saw an airman on the flight deck get run over near the end of the catapult while manning my station. I was hanging out with a fellow sailor who was stationed at bow safety. This was on the end of the catapult right before the metal safety net of the carrier. It was crazy! My shipmate from the flight deck got run over by a plain towing vehicle. Quickly, the ship's medical response team came over and gave him a morphine shot. I will never forget how much pain he seemed to be in. The medical team had to roll a deck plate back from his leg. This is what covers the catapult cylinders. I was really sad for him. It was his first week of his first deployment out to sea and just came aboard. I heard they had to amputate his leg once arriving at the Naval Hospital in San Diego. The accident happened in November 2005, on my final deployment. During that time, I was already furious because someone in administration messed up my citizenship paperwork. In my opinion, we had the worst chief and first class while working on catapults one and two.

    They ordered me to go inside the water breaks. While flight operations were going on! That could have killed me in less than a second if the catapult shot off. These water breaks had hundreds of gallons of water that would stop the pistons from going through the ship. The shuttle was attached to the aircraft and on the verge of launching. The first class and chief told me to look at the water pressure and I knew that was extremely dangerous. The person who was in charge of the operation told me not to do it, so I listened to him. Later, after getting back to home port, the chief took away my blue card. The blue card was so that you could stay out past 12:00 AM

and live out in town. Leaving the USS Kitty Hawk was one of the happiest days of my life, but it has never left me.
~Petty Officer 3rd Class Tom

It goes without saying that veterans who served during war, regardless of designation or rank, will have everlasting trauma. Society is slowly starting to realize that veteran mental health is a major issue. I struggle with thoughts even though it has been almost 20 years since I was in the military. Time doesn't heal all wounds, it only makes them a little more bearable. There are times, even after all of this time, where I think about the number of bombs that were dropped. I think about my part in destroying families' lives. Children that I can't see, mothers I can't hear, and the knowing that there were screams of fear. Fear that we were bombing their homes, marketplaces and historical monuments. As a civilian many years later, I question why we were at war. Why were we fighting something that we didn't understand? I'll never be able to understand it. The thought of all of this can bring me into a morbid state where all I want to do is crumble. I will forever feel ashamed and guilty for the lives we took and the families we obliterated.

Hot Iron

Hidden disabilities stemming from being married and then divorced are real. You name it, physical and mental abuse, alcoholism, drugs, children and so many other factors play a part in mental health within a marriage. According to the website marriage.com, "experts have described relationship trauma as occurring when an intimate relationship has involved significant physical, sexual or psychological abuse."

During my first marriage, I was young and just wrapping up my time in the Navy. I was home on leave getting ready to move to Bremerton, WA. I had just spent the last few years stationed in Yokosuka, Japan, and was excited to get back to the United States. Along with the excitement of being back, I was experiencing major back pains and discomfort in my shoulders and hips. I was also coming from a super intense atmosphere where you were always on alert. I had anger issues, lost control over my emotions, and had very few tools in my toolbelt to know how to handle everything I was going through. Let's also add in the person who I was going to marry and have a couple of kids with was also very young and not ready for motherhood. Statistically, we were a hot mess from the start.

I knew from when I was a kid that I wanted to have lots of children and wanted to be a dad. My mother tells me a story of when I was younger, I was asked what I wanted to be when I grew up, I said, "a dad." That ended up coming much sooner than I would have planned, but fate has a funny way of throwing you into things when you are least expecting it.

While on military leave or what civilians call personal time off, I met Victoria. I wasn't looking for anything serious during that time, but wanted to just have some fun. One night, I was on the website, MySpace, a social application that was one of the pioneers of social media. I ended up talking with the woman who would end up being the mother to my two oldest children. She was just out of basic training and school because she was in the Air National Guard. We started to hang out and roughly six weeks later, we found out we were going to be parents. What did I do besides freak out? Figured I needed to take action, so I arranged a quick wedding for the next weekend. We had a small ceremony with our family and a few friends down in Vancouver, WA. So, there we were. Still finding out who each other were, pregnant, young AND I was about to go on a deployment. Almost every obstacle that you could throw at us, we had.

The first year we were married essentially set the stage for the next years to come. High stress, ill-equipped with the tools we needed to be successful, and I was also dealing with serious post-traumatic stress and many physical pains at the time. She didn't have a smooth pregnancy either. She was quickly diagnosed with preeclampsia and was extremely sick the entire time. We were trying to navigate so many things and it often ended with huge fighting matches. I acted just like my parents and yelled and used my size to try and intimidate when I would verbally fight. It was a constant battle and how we handled those fights was not healthy. What did we do? We just buried the feelings inside and always just moved on like nothing happened. As I have gotten older, I know that is one of the worst ways to deal with issues.

We ended up moving back home to Klamath Falls, OR. When I got out of the Navy, a few months after my oldest was born. I was going to start college and figure out a new life outside of the military whilst navigating having a new baby and marrying someone I hardly knew. As years went by, we ended up having another baby. That didn't help the heaps of differences we had and the arguments worsened. There were a couple of times where Victoria got physical. This was extremely hard to go through and during her flare-ups, I would feel the same way I did when I was a child getting yelled at. This is known as C.P.T.S.D or Complex Post Traumatic Stress Disorder.

CPTSD

Complex post-traumatic stress disorder (CPTSD, C-PTSD or cPTSD) is a mental health condition that can develop if you experience chronic (long-term) trauma. It involves stress responses, such as:

- Anxiety.
- Having flashbacks or nightmares.
- Avoiding situations, places and other things related to the traumatic event.
- Heightened emotional responses, such as impulsivity or aggressiveness.
- Persistent difficulties in sustaining relationships.

Examples of chronic trauma include:

- Long-term child physical or sexual abuse.
- Long-term domestic violence.
- Being a victim of human or sex trafficking.
- War.
- Frequent community violence.

The fear had internally sent me back to feeling small. It felt like a dark force, almost as if you could see it start at your feet and watch it slowly creep up your body. My heart and chest would feel heavy as if someone was pushing me down on me with a large cement stone. During times like that, I would mentally check out.

I didn't grow up being physically abused, so I didn't know how to react when it happened to me. We were in an argument and my friend was staying with us at the time. He was directly across from us in the other room while we were having a huge disagreement. Out of nowhere, she swung and punched me in the jaw. It was like slow motion and I couldn't stop it. I was in shock. With the exception of being in a fight with a friend or foe in the past, this was my spouse.

At that point I stepped back and really started to evaluate what had just happened and what I was doing, but even though I knew that this behavior was toxic, I stayed. Of course, I then endured more abuse. During one confrontation she was ironing something and got extremely angry and threw the hot iron at me. With my cat-like reflexes, I dodged the scolding hot iron and decided it was time to take a walk. Reflecting on those times I often ask myself, "Why did I stay for so long?" The answer was that I was terrified of losing my two kids. I had heard so many times that the chances of a dad getting custody was extremely small. Again, being a young adult, I didn't know much about it. All I knew is that I wanted to be there for my kids.

As months turned into a few years, we moved to Anchorage, AK, because she had military orders. We thought that it would be a great change of pace and I had always wanted to explore the Alaskan wilderness. In a few short months, we were off to Alaska and leaving behind friends and family. Her sister's family was going to live in the Oregon house while we were in Alaska for a few years. Everything was set and off we went, but hurt, confusion, and a massive life change was coming.

After a few short months and having moved over 3,000 miles away, she said she wanted a divorce. There I was, making very little money and knowing just a few people, and all of my insecurities and doubts emerged. I had stopped going to college with one semester to go because I wanted to move and get settled. The job I had paid very little and I had no clue how I was going to make it. Anchorage was a tough place to find myself and, at the time, was the second most expensive city to live in after Honolulu, Hawaii. I didn't have any friends and was in a mental state that was all over the place. And even though in the back of my head I knew that the divorce was about to happen, I was still shocked.

I immediately called my parents and told them what had happened. It wasn't a feeling of loss yet, but I was scared of what my life was going to be like. It was winter in Alaska.

Dark for 18 hours at a time, cold and a perfect feeding ground for depression and anxiety. All of my insecurities and fears were coming back to me. Over five years of my life were in turmoil and I had a hard time seeing past the gloom. I went into a deep depression and felt isolated in my own skin. At the time, my only release was alcohol and writing. Sad but true, I didn't know what else to do. I couldn't go back home. I was afraid of losing my children. I was broke and couldn't afford to rent a nice place. My life had come crashing down and it took a few years to get back to myself.

The first Christmas I had without my kids was awful. This was the first time that I wouldn't be with my children for a holiday. I was as low as it could get. I was alone on Christmas and had nowhere to go. I ended up with a buddy at a bar. In a few short hours I was drunk, trying to escape reality for a bit, but that was one of the worst things that I could have done. That night I slept outside on a bench for a while before someone asked if I was okay. I said yes, but clearly my face didn't look like I was okay. I found my way home, but it was a blur.

Right after the divorce, I went on a guided fishing trip in Seward, AK. I was super distraught at that time and had a hard time talking about what was going on. I don't like surprises. Anyone that knows me, will tell you that I love routine. Not to say that I can't be spontaneous at times, but generally I like to know what is going on. After spending the night in a yurt, I woke up early and got on the chartered boat. We sailed off into the harbor looking for halibut and lingcod. We were out for a while and I started to talk to a few folks that were on the boat. One man could tell that I was going through some things. My guess is that my face told the story well, as I have always had a hard time hiding my emotions when something is really bothering me. We started chatting for a while and of course I brought up why I was there. He told me he had gone through some of the same things and also got divorced young without much support. One thing he told me that I've remembered ever since, and was so true. He said to take the total number of years you were married and cut that in half, and that would be about how long it would take to really move on. At the time, I took what he said with a grain of salt, and kept moving on. That day ended with a smile as I caught multiple lingcod and halibut to fill the freezer.

  Time started to pass, but I was in a constant state of worry and anger. I wasn't angry because of the divorce, I was angry that I was now trapped in Anchorage and had no control over leaving. Because of this, I forced myself to find some light in the dark. Employment became steady and in time I started to find a few friends. They were all about the same age and new to Alaska as well. A few of us really started to bond and I found a pack. There were about four of us who hung out most of the time. I tried not to have them too involved with what I was going through and hid most of what I was going through with alcohol and random one night stands. I was in a dark place mentally and felt like I had no outlet, no release of the pain and fear.

For months, I would go to the bar and sleep with almost any female who would have me. I never had a relationship and wanted nothing to do with one. I was reckless with women and was trying to find comfort anywhere. It was dangerous and I got myself into some situations where I was lucky to have made it home. This had gone on for a couple of years until I moved back to Oregon.

For years, I didn't ever want to get married again or commit myself to anyone other than my kids. This all changed when I met Meredith. Something that I would always say after my divorce was, I just want someone who will help me out 10% of the time. What I experienced during those five years of marriage with Victoria made me convinced that I would always have to do all of the work. I couldn't accept that another partner would give any more than what I had already experienced. Years of reflecting on that marriage, I should have never been married to Victoria. Red flags were abundant, but I wouldn't acknowledge them. Instead, I suffered in silence. Meredith, my wife, has shown me what a partnership really looks like. It is not always 50/50, but we do our best to balance everything in the end. Meredith was the person I had been looking for, and she fills my bucket daily.

Over the course of mine and Meredith's ten-year relationship, I have slipped into my old ways a handful of times. I have yelled at her, scared her, and used my size and big voice to try and intimidate her. It has been so bad at times that she has said she was going to leave me. Honestly, I wouldn't have blamed her if she did. Although I have worked hard not to act in ways that were modeled to me, I still slip up. There is an internal switch that turns on when all of my fear and anxiety rear its ugly head. Realistically, it doesn't matter how I was treated when I was young. Meredith does not deserve to experience anything but love from me. Her partner. Her husband. Her best friend.

While the time passes and I continue to learn, I have to continuously try and be the best partner that I can. Counseling is going to help, but there is much more work to do. I am not able to stop working at it. Working through these issues I have will be a lifelong journey. Creeping back into old behaviors can't happen. If it does, divorce number two will surely happen. I can't let my past dictate my future.

Many people experience all sorts of trauma prior to divorce, during divorce, and post-divorce. Life is changing, kids are dealing with it, and although you might have been through a divorce as well, your experience is not their experience. Support looks different for every person. By looking at a person, you can't tell what trauma they have faced during their marriage. The best thing someone can do during a time like this is to be a good listener. Many of the emotions that person is experiencing are very confusing. The trauma from the marriage and during the divorce can take a toll on anyone, even without any disabilities. Add in years of trauma and abuse? This will create a massive avalanche of unknowns. When you hear of a person going through a tough marriage and then a divorce, don't try and give them advice. Your story is not their story. Be a sounding board and only give suggestions if they ask for them. Let them speak freely without judgment. This is what they need.

Change the Narrative

Over the last 17 years, I have had the pleasure to be the father to four amazing children, two with Victoria, and two with my wife Meredith. The difficulties of having trauma as a kid are that you are bound to repeat some of those mistakes. It's common sense. Monkey see, monkey do. Now, that doesn't mean that the narrative can't change, and that is what I have worked hard to do. It hasn't been easy. Nor am I done making dramatic changes.

As previously mentioned, my first marriage did not work out and there were many reasons for that. In those five years, however, I was blessed to have my first two children. I often tell my oldest son that he saved my life. No matter how old he gets, or how my memory will fade, I always want him to remember that. Through the hard times as well as the good, I want him to know he has a separate part of my life that none of the other children do. As he has grown, I have grown as a man and a parent. Things have never been easy for us, with constant moving and our world disrupted more times than a young boy should go through.

Right before I knew I was going to be a dad, I was partying hard in the military. I was reckless. I had been living in

Japan for a few years and we got into some heavy drugs plus I was drinking daily to cope with my issues. I was young and afraid to reach out for help. I took cocaine, ecstasy, methamphetamines and so many other unnamed drugs that were available in Japan at the time. Too many of my brothers and sisters never recovered from our substance abuse. My time was almost up on my orders to be in Japan and I was getting ready to transfer to Bremerton, WA. It was at that time that I told myself as soon as I got back into the states, I would stop all of the drug usage, fighting, and other nonsense I was involved with.

After my tour was over in Yokosuka, I ended back in Klamath Falls, OR. I had 30 days of military leave, or in civilian terms, personal time off (PTO). At the age of 22 with a head full of steam, I was looking for fun and women. I was a United States Sailor and full of myself. The military has a way of giving you a sense of confidence that is also accompanied by a large ego. I met a girl online which was a new thing at the time. I wasn't looking for a relationship. During that time I was trying to have a good time and ship out to my next duty station.

All of that changed in a matter of months. There I was sitting in my apartment in Bremerton, WA without a care in the world. Only thing I had to worry about was taking care of myself and getting to the ship on time. The night before? I was out at a bar and got into a fight and fled the scene to get back home before the police showed up. Not a good situation. My girlfriend, who eventually became my first wife, called and my heart stopped. She said, I am pregnant. Full stop. My world just came to a screeching halt and the world became much more complicated. In fact, I was planning on breaking up with her that week. I was planning on meeting my ex-girlfriend from high school the following weekend to reconnect. After a few days of chaos, we decided to get married a week later to make sure she was covered for health insurance and we would be eligible for a place to live on the base. Was that the best move? Not even a little bit, but I was young and panicked.

Months went by and I cleaned up my act, for the most part. We were expecting a little boy and I was extremely excited. Although the situation was not ideal, we were attempting to make it work. One of the major issues is that I not only had no clue how to be a parent, but I was also suffering from PTSD and severe anxiety from my military service. I couldn't sleep and had nightmares most nights. Amongst the chaos, I was holding on by a string. My wife and I would argue and yell. She was young and her world was rocked as well. One thing I always knew though, I was going to be a dad. Gone were the days where I had to think of only myself, but now I had a new purpose.

My son was born in a traumatic fashion as his mom was life flighted to a hospital after a routine check and they found out that she had eclampsia. The baby came four weeks earlier than expected and we were not ready. Our life had changed, and the world kept moving forward, but that didn't stop all of the mental issues that were occurring. Having the baby just masked and distracted the monster inside my head. It would rear its ugly head soon enough. I had stopped doing any drugs, but I would still drink too much and was headed on a path of alcoholism. Luckily, that didn't happen. If it wasn't for my son, I am not sure I would have had the strength to come out of what I was doing.

A couple of years went by and we had another baby. A daughter. She had big beautiful brown eyes that just captured your heart as soon as you glanced at her. At that time, Victoria and I were not doing well. Everything we did was masked behind the kids, work and college. We would fight and disagree to the point of extreme yelling. The saddest part? Much of this was done in front of the kids. They were now experiencing what I never wanted. I was repeating the cycle.

During this time when the kids were little, Victoria received orders to Alaska and so we thought that would be a good restart. This time period was short lived, as we soon got divorced and I became a single father. My world as a single father was just beginning. My kids were caught in the middle and to no fault of their own, experiencing their own anxieties due to all of the fighting. They witnessed their mom and dad full-fledged yelling. I am thankful that they never saw the iron that was thrown at me or their mom punching me. I'm sure that would have had everlasting memories. My memories of witnessing events of my parent's have never gone away. They are burned into my brain and I am thankful that my kids didn't have to witness the abuse.

When we moved to Alaska, the kids were two and four years old. Barely old enough to remember anything now. I have asked them if they remember much of those days, and they don't remember much. I am thankful for that.

After a divorce and an extremely difficult time in Alaska, we were finally able to move back to Oregon. We only spent a short time there until we had the opportunity to move up to Vancouver, WA. We were able to settle in and before too long, I met my future, Meredith.

Challenges were still upon me when it came to learning how to be a parent. The work of making change is never ending, and I will always strive to be better. With that said, I can look back on things that I chose to do as a parent that I am not proud of. Discipline when I was a child was yelling from my parents that led to isolating myself in my room or gym. Before meeting Meredith, I thought that I was doing mostly everything right. I had really gotten better at raising my voice and using threatening language towards my kids, but not perfect. Instead of yelling, I would do other things that I thought were "okay". Later, I found out that what I was doing was also abusive behavior. If my kids were misbehaving I would have them put their hands up on a wall over their head while keeping their nose on the wall. This could last anywhere from a few minutes or longer. I wasn't yelling or hitting them, so it was okay, right? Wrong. Dead wrong. Other times, I would use intimidation by clapping really loudly at them. Scaring them. Making them know I was big and scary. Thinking about it years later, it makes me want to sit in a dark room and cry. Those actions will forever be ingrained in their mind. Images of their dad making them feel anything but safe. This was an absolute failure as a parent.

    Since that time, I have grown and learned a variety of parenting skills that are much healthier. Learning moments and realizing sometimes, kids are just kids. They learn by making mistakes. How we handle those mistakes will either provide confidence or uncertainty in our children.

I met Meredith at work and we often had long talks in both my office and hers. We are ten years of age apart, but we both found that we connected even though we were extremely different. We officially started dating in October of 2015 and a short five months later she was pregnant with my third child. Again, I was in shock, but was much older than the first time I found out I was going to be a father. Even with that, I was nervous about our situation. We had only been dating a short time and now we were going to have a child. A substantial difference this time was that I was in love with her and we had already talked about kids and our future life. Everything just sped up.

In December of 2016 my third child was born. Excitement and fear went on internally and my emotions were running rampant. Many thoughts came to me during that time. How was this going to be different than the first time I was going to be a father? I had been in survival mode for so long that I couldn't understand how fatherhood was going to be different. First time around I had to take care of the kids alone for much of the time. I bounced from job to job trying to make ends meet. My insecurities of the past would set in from time to time. Although I had a supportive partner, it didn't stop the fears and thoughts that this, too, was going to be extremely difficult.

My parenting skills were inadequate. This is something that I will always need to work on. Know better, do better. I knew how to be a father, but had struggled with regulating my emotions. I was emotionally vulnerable and had not worked through many of my own mental struggles with parenthood. Life had always been hard when it came to parenthood. Nothing with my two older children came easy. I had to learn that things could change, but it was going to take a lot of work. Most of that work didn't come until I was able to look inward. Even though my partner is an extremely wonderful mother and supportive partner, that didn't change who I was.

When I was a child, yelling was normal. Controlling emotions when things got tough was not something I learned. I knew that I had internal anger issues and had a short fuse when it came to being elevated. Punching and kicking walls near my childhood bedroom still remain in my memory all these years later, a sad reminder of my past as a child. Trauma from the past had ultimately given me doubts about my own ability to be a great parent.

A couple of years later, we had established our family routine and were wanting to expand our family. Meredith and I knew that we loved each other and were blessed with a baby girl. This was one of the most special days of my life. The nurse asked me if I wanted to deliver my baby. I had already had three other kiddos, but I was able to deliver her. It was a life-changing experience. My mind was focused and the only fear I had during that was *not* to drop her. At that moment, nothing else in the world mattered but her. It was exhilarating.

With an open mind and willingness to change the ways that I had parented before, Meredith stuck by my side. Why does all of this relate to trauma and hidden disabilities? Mental issues stem from past experiences. They are often handed down from generation to generation. We have the ability to modify the behaviors we have learned and trauma that we have experienced. As parents, we don't have to continue the cycle that has been handed down to us. After 17 years of parenthood and not dealing with my own trauma or addressing it, I made the decision to go to therapy and talk about why I was the way I was, and how I thought about things and why I acted in a way I was not proud of. Today, although I have gotten much better at regulating my emotions, it is still something I have to work on daily.

Not all children escape from trauma, and my oldest two children are no exception. Early in my daughter's life, she had been to five different schools in six years. My son had been to four. New friends, new teachers, and learning new rules and regulations became a very normal thing. My two older kids are now masters at adapting and mostly overcoming obstacles and transitions. As good as they are, they both struggle with a few hidden disabilities themselves. Early in their life, it was traumatic and the only thing that was stable in their life was me and each other.

Several times during their lives, their mother left. Once when they were one and three years old. To this day, I am not sure she left because she was told or that she wanted to. Regardless of that, I had both toddlers by myself and was about to head on a journey. During that time, we were stressed and had very little communication with their mom. Sometimes we would go over a week without communication. This was the first time that my kids faced a parent being gone from the home for that long. They were little enough not to be too affected by it, but it was extremely difficult for them. Years later, they were dropped off on Thanksgiving week with black plastic trash bags filled with clothes and other belongings. Victoria was leaving, and they had no idea when she was going to be back. I had also been laid off just a week before and had no idea how I was going to make it.

Thank goodness Meredith was there! I even gave her the option to end the relationship. We were newly dating and I was about to be a full time father, again. Life was going to drastically change and I understood if she didn't want to be involved in that. At that moment, I knew I loved her, and would have been devastated if she left.

Meredith and I figured out as much of a plan that we could. I had been a single parent before, but Meredith was jumping in with two feet in the fire. The next two years we answered questions as to why the kids mom wasn't there. Questions about when she is going to come back. Their mom tried to come up every once in a while, but it was sometimes weeks at a time. There was no clear timeline on when she would return, so the kids were constantly in a state of wonder. Each time that their mom would see them, she would leave and the tears would come back for a few days. I couldn't explain to them what was going on, simply because I didn't know anymore than they did.

Not knowing when you will see or hear from a parent is hard for kids. When children cry when their parents leave them when they are young, life stalls. A fear almost always happens that the parent who is missing may never come back. Nature with parents, more with mothers, says that we will be protected until we are able to handle the outside world on our own. Victoria's leaving and not communicating a return caused symptoms that are similar to separation anxiety.

A couple of years had passed and Victoria said that she was moving back to the area. This was extremely difficult to navigate. There were so many emotions that the kids were going through, we just tried to stay supportive. Their routine was completely out of sync. They were again now traveling back and forth every other week from my house to Victoria's.

When you have severe anxiety mixed with chronic depression, as a parent, it can consume you. That time period was exhausting, but worth every second. We all had to learn to work with each other. Good times and bad, we were there and had to assimilate.

I am not going to sit here and tell you that I don't have my breakdowns and recurring issues. Meredith has to tell me at times to lower my tone and not be so intense. She knows where it is coming from, but it doesn't matter. I can't repeat what happened to myself as well as what I did to my oldest children. It used to be that I had to constantly think about what I was going to say and how I was going to react. Now, I do my best to calm down. One thing that I have had to do was learn what battles I was willing to fight for. Meredith will tell me, Max, does "enter a situation" really matter? Pick your battles, she says. I now take this very seriously and bring those words into teaching and other avenues in my life. I am a work in progress, but I am doing everything I can to change the narrative.

Throat Punch

From the military to the public and private sectors, I have experienced abuse and it took me years to realize it. Once I did, my eyes opened up to all of the situations people are in where abuse is happening. All emotional abuse can be avoided, full stop. There are protections against discrimination and abuse, yet many companies and organizations don't follow the law. What is even worse is that some have been so conditioned to it, that they don't even know they are doing it or a victim of it.

Workplace trauma has been around for generations stemming clear back to the beginning of humanity. Abuse in the workplace can come from a variety of places. Coworkers, employees and supervisors are all in positions to receive and dish out harmful experiences.

Many people don't talk about the subject in fear of being fired or let go. The system has failed us. Power and ego have caused us to turn on each other and society has just become immune to it. Most people are in the workplace more than they are in their own homes. They spend more time with co-workers than they do their own family. The workplace should be a safe place for people to go without fear of being harassed and made to feel anything other than good. Unfortunately, this isn't always the case.

This is a problem in every sector of work. The private sector, public, military and non-profit world, people are affected in different ways. We have all heard the saying, "Sticks and stones may break my bones, but words will not hurt me." That statement is wrong and completely out of touch with how we operate as humans. We have been told for ages that what people say to us shouldn't affect us and we should just move on. One of the major issues with this is that people ARE affected and words do hurt.

Psychology Today defines abuse as, "An isolated occurrence doesn't necessarily qualify as emotional abuse, but a pattern of behavior that creates fear and control does. Such mistreatment can occur in a range of interpersonal contexts including a parental relationship, romantic relationship or a professional relationship." In some cases, emotional abuse can have a much longer effect on people than physical abuse. This is because emotional abuse gets behind someone's psyche. The pain can take years to surface and even longer to heal from. For many people, the pain will never fully go away. They just learn to cope with their trauma.

Let's start off with the military. Yes, the military is filled with emotional abuse from top to bottom. How do I know? I have experienced it and witnessed it during the five years that I served. From the time I signed on the dotted line, the emotional abuse started. We were treated less than human and made to feel like we were subjects. I understand that the military is training young men and women for the worst case scenario: war. This doesn't change how the negative and harmful behavior affects each service member.

    I remember the first night I was in bootcamp and getting assigned to my barracks. When you first get off the bus, you are shoveled like mice into a warehouse. You are stripped of anything and everything you have and expected to keep your head cool while being yelled at. One of the stations that you have to go through is to be drug tested. As I made my way to the urinal, I was shaking and my anxiety level was at an all time high. I did what I was asked and after filling the cup, my hands shook and I dropped the cup back into the urinal. At that moment, I felt like dying. I walked up to the Petty Officers in charge and told them what happened. That's the first time I had ever been terrified in the workplace. A senior officer started to yell at me and said some horrific things, all because I dropped the cup because I was so nervous. After getting ridiculed in front of hundreds of new sailors, I was told to run around the warehouse and to drink water at every station possible. Because of the nerves and already depleting what fluid I had left in me, I was running around the warehouse for what felt like hours. Each lap I was yelled at. Each lap I became more stressed, making it even harder to do what I needed to do. Each lap I asked myself over and over what in the hell did I get myself into. Eventually, I consumed so much water that I was finally able to go to the bathroom again. I was able to hold on to that cup with dear life this time. The military has some archaic practices and has the mentality that "this is how it has always been done." Other branches have similar practices and emotional abuse continues throughout your enlistment.

After the military was over, I didn't go straight into the workforce. I had major pain in my back and other physical issues that prevented me from doing much at the time. Instead, I decided to go back to college and see where that took me. For much of that time, I struggled with class. I couldn't remember anything. I couldn't understand things that seemed simple to other students. After my first year of struggling, I talked to one of my professors. He had done research on head injuries and thought that something could be going on. I took what he said seriously and went to the Veterans Affairs hospital and told them what had been going on. After a three-day testing cycle, they found out that I had incurred major brain trauma. Doctors told me that I had spots of brain damage from a variety of head traumas. My frontal cortex and the amygdala, had been affected and my ability to remember things became extremely difficult. Not only was I dealing with that, but also undiagnosed PTSD, Anxiety and Depression. I was later diagnosed after seeking treatment. This was my first experience with a disability, but I had no clue it would affect me for years to come with employers.

My first substantial abuse came from an employer in the real estate industry. For confidentiality, I won't bring the name of the company into the story. The year was 2020 and I had been out of work due to the COVID pandemic. Recruiters, which was the role I was in, were some of the first people who were let go. When companies become uncertain, they would typically let go of recruiters and sales employees. I had been unemployed for four months and was desperate for employment. I have been the sole financial supporter for my family and we were barely getting by. I worked with a recruiting agency and they found a recruiting role for this company. I was excited that I was going to get into a new industry and liked the challenge of recruiting real estate professionals to come join this national brand. Unfortunately, I would soon find out that I was in for one of the worst professional experiences that I had since getting out of the military.

I had started the position with big hopes of making it in the industry. The people I was working with seemed great and all were doing well in their career. I started my training and started to make progress. I had recruited a handful of new agents to the office and had a good pipeline of folks to interview. This was no easy task, I found out. It turned out that many people couldn't stand the company I was working for. They let me know about how bad the company had treated them previous to me calling them. At the time, I didn't think much about it. It was typical for people to be a bit disgruntled after leaving a company, but most of these folks were next-level upset. Almost instantly when I mentioned where I was calling from, I could feel the anger through the phone.

After being there for a few months, I knew that something was wrong. My boss, or "team leader" in that industry, had it in her head that it was okay to make fun of other employees and considered that a way of building camaraderie. This also included texting the group completely unethical and sexual comments on a group text feed. I refused and told her I didn't feel comfortable doing that. Why did she justify behaving this way? Because she said that was the way she was brought up in the industry. This also included yelling at her employees and making sure we all knew who was the boss. Over time the yelling and mistreatment escalated during the next couple of months and I would come home defeated. Then there was an event that made me not only leave, but leave by sending an email on a Sunday night before I was supposed to go back into the office.

One morning, I got into my office, which was directly connected via a door to my boss's office. The idea behind the close quarters was that she could easily train me and listen to the calls I was making. That week, she reminded me that I was getting close to being paid primarily on commission and my base pay was going to drop. I was sitting at my desk and she called me over to do some impromptu training. I had forgotten to bring in my backpack with my notepads in it. To save time from running out to my car, I just grabbed a piece of scratch paper. In my head, this was acceptable and figured I would just transfer what notes I had taken to either my computer or other notepad. Boy was I wrong. I sat down at a round table in her office with another employee also taking notes. After sitting down with my scratch paper to take down some notes, my boss exploded. It was like watching the ocean turn violent in minutes. She said, "How in the hell are you going to take notes on scratch paper!?! What would Gary Keller think!?! Go get your laptop!" I was in complete shock and my anxiety and most of my psychological issues instantly came to the forefront. I was sweating and calmly told her that I didn't have a laptop and was never issued one. My standard notepad was in my car, (so I hoped). After that she said, "I should THROAT PUNCH you!" When I feel threatened or anxious, I smile. I don't realize I am doing it. I will also almost laugh, not because I find the situation funny, but because that is my body's response to that stressor. Fortunately, we were still wearing masks and she could not see what was happening underneath. Those words carried into the hallway. She told me that I needed to go out and get that notepad and come right back. At that moment, I felt like I did when I was a young child. It was yet another real experience with Complex Post Traumatic Stress Disorder.

As I walked out to my car, I couldn't help to think what would happen if I had forgotten my backpack. What would I do? The world had just crashed down on me and I felt hopeless. Never had I felt such hostility in the civilian workplace. Even in the military I never received anything that came close to that. In the military, you do get yelled at, but there is usually something extremely dangerous or could something that is life threatening involved. This was just a real estate office. No one was going to die. No one was going to spend their career there. My thought was simple. If my backpack was not in my car, I was going to get in and drive home. Imagine standing in front of a mountain lion standing still looking at you while crouching down ready to pounce. The fear radiated through my body of what could happen coming back empty handed. I didn't want to face her again, at all, ever. I pulled my keys out of my pocket and opened the passenger door to my Jeep. Looked in and panicked because it wasn't where I usually keep it. My body felt weak, as if you are hugging the toilet while vomiting. I then opened that back door and looked behind the seat. Thank goodness it was there! I walked back into the office and sat down while shaking and terrified. Hands wet with precipitation and my body feeling as if I had been a blistering sunburn. All of the information that she was talking about wasn't coming in clear. I was distraught and my fight or flight response was on overdrive. She didn't apologize, but told me that she "thought" I could handle the treatment because I had the look. She said that I was big, tattooed and ex-military, so she assumed I was used to that kind of treatment. The day ended and I couldn't wait to get home to Meredith.

As I was driving home, I thought about the day. How was I supposed to go back to the office after being treated like that? It was a Thursday and after talking to my wife, we decided I was going to quit. I felt a sense of relief and went in the next day knowing it would be my last. Over that weekend, we crafted an email and waited until Sunday night to send it. There was no way I was going to go back to the office and give two weeks. They didn't deserve it and I could only imagine the yelling and abuse that would come if I did it in person. First time I have ever quit a job like that and I had zero remorse. Here is the email:

I'm resigning from my position of Recruiter effective immediately.

My resignation is due to a series of incidents that have occurred in my three months at this office. I have been physically threatened by my immediate supervisor, Beatrice, who told me she should "throat punch" me for not bringing a notebook to a meeting, which was witnessed by my colleague. I have also both witnessed and heard colleagues being yelled at and belittled, as well as been the recipient of both belittling and yelling from my supervisor. I have also heard derogatory remarks amongst the staff, read multiple sexual and discriminatory messages on group text feeds and messenger feeds between colleagues and my supervisor, and have been encouraged by my supervisor to "pick a colleague to make fun of" in order to fit in. My discomfort and reluctance to do so was met with my supervisor choosing our human resource staff as a suggested target.

When I expressed discomfort with these things, I was told by my direct supervisor that I was making my colleagues uncomfortable and that they "don't know how to act" in front of me.

In my twenty years of work experience in various fields, I have never neglected giving an employer a two week notice upon resignation, nor resigned over email. But, because of the incidents and situations listed above, I do not feel comfortable or safe from retaliatory behavior if I were to resign any other way.

After going through that, I wanted to never be treated like that again. Little did I know that I would experience discrimination because of my disabilities just a short time later.

There I was, looking for employment again, and by this point I was used to the cycle of recruiting. Times are good when things are good, but when they are bad, you lose a job. There was a company that I had been eyeing for several years and thought if I could make it there, I had hit recruiting gold. This company was in one of the tallest buildings in downtown Portland, OR and known to be an amazing place to work. For years, I looked at the building and thought, "I will work there someday." That day came after a friend said they were looking for a new recruiter and he thought that I would be a great fit. I had interviewed with him a few years before this, but had applied to a position I was overqualified for.

The interview process started and I had a wonderful experience. Everything that I imagined about the company seemed true. The people, the environment and culture were all on par with everything I heard. Soon I was hired and was thrilled to finally be working in a company I had admired for years. COVID was still keeping many people at home, so I was working from home.

In the next few months, I worked on building my pipeline of candidates and got to know the hiring managers I was working with. This was pretty standard practice when starting out as a new recruiter. My requisition (job) load was starting to increase as I was doing well with what I had been working with. My boss would let me know that hiring managers loved working with me. Those first few months were what I wanted them to be. I was recruiting high level tech professionals and meeting my goals. Because of that, I was asked to work with more requisitions and gladly accepted those.

Over the years, I had always learned to cope with my disabilities. I had gone to college, been successful in a variety of roles and found ways to process information. My loss of short-term memory typically affected me more than other things. With that said, my anxiety would flare up when I couldn't remember something because I didn't want to disappoint who I was working with. As I acquired new requisitions, the job seemed to get much harder. I was fully remote and my supervisor lived on the East Coast and worked those hours.

After some time, I was getting behind and not doing nearly as well as I had previously been doing. I had total awareness of what was going on, but I felt the anxiety starting to build. I was well aware that my performance was starting to slip, but didn't have the confidence to say anything about it. This went on for a while and my supervisor started to become impatient and upset with me. After speaking to my wife, we decided that it would be best if I disclose my disability and ask for an accommodation. I loved where I was working and didn't want my disabilities to get in the way of that. I talked to my employer about my disability and that I needed an accommodation. For the first time in my career, I disclosed to my employer the struggles I had and admitted that I needed help. My ego and confidence had never been in line with letting any employer know about it and never wanted to be looked at differently than anyone else. When addressing what was going on, I asked for what I thought would be a simple request. I asked for more verbal communication from my boss. With everything being done each week through numerous emails, messaging groups and one-on-ones, I had a hard time remembering things. I took notes, but at times I had forgotten what they meant. Everything came in so fast I felt completely overwhelmed. I knew I needed direct communication so that I could unjumble my thoughts and find clarity with my work.

According to the American Disabilities Act, (ADA) Title 1, "It restricts questions that can be asked about applicants' disability before a job offer is made and requires that employers make reasonable accommodations to the known physical or mental limitations of otherwise qualified individuals with disabilities unless it results in undue hardship."

I was told that I had to take a paid leave of absence while they went through the process. In the next couple of weeks I talked to multiple people from the disability investigation and worked closely with one of the companies Human Resource Business Partners (HRBP). The process took much longer than I had expected. I had to pull up records showing my disability and that it was from military service. Pages of documents were pulled and sent to the investigating party. After everything was submitted, I waited for the decision to come back. Never in my wildest dreams did I expect the overall outcome.

What had started as a simple ask turned into a full fledged investigation. Stress and anxiety built up because I was unclear that I was at risk of losing my job. I had put myself in an extremely vulnerable position that I had never been in before. After six weeks of being in the dark and the investigation looming, I received an email with the HRBP and my supervisor. My insides were turning. A lump sat in my throat and perspiration covered my body. As soon as the Zoom video meeting started, I knew that it wasn't going to be good. The supervisor and HRBP had serious looks on their faces.

In the next few minutes, the sky felt like it not only fell on me, but crushed my soul at the same time. My supervisor and HRBP said that they were unable to accommodate my disability request. The solution? I was offered a severance package that stated I was unable to pursue legal action and that they were going to pay me for the next six weeks. How generous I thought. My dream company was paying me to *not* speak up while disregarding my request. At the time I was crushed and extremely embarrassed. I could have chosen to not sign the severance, but I needed the money to take care of my family.

Despite this most recent traumatic experience, time started to move on and I eventually found a new position. As a matter of fact, the new position was amazing. I worked for an aerospace company with a solid team. After having such a terrible ending to the last position, I was hesitant to bring up anything about my disability. A good friend of mine who referred me to the position told me I should absolutely tell the director about what I needed. He was right. I spoke to my director and talked about how I could be successful. After speaking to him, he said it was a no-brainer. Whatever I needed to be successful, he would accommodate. Unfortunately, after 16 months that company started to have financial troubles and most of our team was let go. Although I again was laid off, this company showed compassion for what I had gone through. I was a top performer and had nothing but great performance reviews. All of this was done with a simple accommodation.

Another professional who has experienced workplace trauma is my friend Suzie. She has been an executive in the workplace working in human resources. Once Suzie heard about what I was writing, she wanted to share her experience as well.

Suzie Schweitzer~

When I first heard about invisible disabilities, I was working for a tech company where I was responsible for arranging impact speakers for employee engagement. I had recently finished my run as the President of our local SHRM chapter (Society of Human Resources) and the Director of the State SHRM chapter mentioned that she was providing a speech on Invisible Disabilities free of charge to companies. In the back of my mind, I thought, "Maybe it will apply to a small group of employees and will be worthwhile for them." To my amazement, almost every single person in the building at my company showed up, eagerly participated, and stayed behind afterwards to share tidbits about their own struggles, thoughts, observations. I was shocked at how vital and previously uncovered this topic was for our employees. Many of them shared they were struggling privately, not knowing who to turn to, or whether to reveal their conditions at all. In my 15+ years working in HR, I've seen my share of accommodations requests, however hearing from my long term colleagues about how they didn't feel safe to share their disabilities with our company was eye opening. Many of the suggestions were simple, in that they needed an ergonomic adjustment to a machine, or more understanding to what it is like being neurodivergent. These employees were highly paid

R&D engineers. High functioning and highly valued in society. Yet, they knew intellectually that being open about disabilities is still taboo. I, too, was secretly hiding my struggles, however I didn't know that I would technically qualify as someone with a disability. At the time, I knew I was struggling with a few things, however I did not know I had my own BIG invisible disability that I was ignoring, but I would soon find out. Underlining all of this is an unspoken rule that HR cannot disclose personal information yet, we see behind the scenes and often hide our own. When I complete an EEOC statement in a job application, I have learned not to be too open about my own identities. I cringe to say it, but I've seen far too many HR professionals and business leaders who have not done the work to gain understanding or unpack their own unconscious bias and truthfully you never know what a company is doing with that information. Different companies have different styles of storing and sharing the information and it is not protected in the same way that PHI (Personal Health Information) or HIPAA information is. People are bound to assume the worst when they see that someone has marked the box for disabilities and instead of asking and going through the interactive process, it's too easy for the individual screening applications to write off the individual as a 'problem'

applicant or they may even completely assume the person does not meet the physical qualifications of the job.
~Suzie Schweitzer

These situations are not typical, but happen more than most people think. In fact, I truly believe that there is much more discrimination in the workplace than we even know about. People are afraid to lose their jobs, security and feel if they speak up, they will be let go. It happens, so why wouldn't they be scared? There are people in the world who are in positions of power. They push around their status and don't think about how their actions could affect others.

Over the past couple of years, I have had some great experiences in the workplace. The aerospace company I worked for was fun and my manager was incredible. Even though I was let go on a mass layoff, I look back fondly on that experience and how my manager didn't shame me for my disability, but embraced it and tried to understand what it was that I needed. If you read this, thank you Rob.

After getting out of the corporate world this past year and into education, I question at times if I will experience similar situations that I have in the past. Post Traumatic Stress Disorder rears its ugly head when it wants to. People who have not experienced it sometimes cannot understand how these intrusive thoughts can destroy someone's way of thinking.

    I will always be tentative when working with superiors. The awful experiences that I have gone through will stay with me. No matter how much therapy and success that I have in the future, I will always think about those companies that allowed their managers to treat me the way they did.

Olive

Let's face it. You see a service dog and you automatically assume its owner is disabled. Right? If you don't, you are a rare one. People have many opinions, but many don't actually know what a service dog is or what distinguishes a dog as a service dog.

Service Dog:
Service animals are defined as dogs that are individually trained to do work or perform tasks for people with disabilities.

My beautiful service dog's name is Olive. Olive is a Rottweiler and has been in a training program since she was born. When I first brought her home, she was eight weeks old and absolutely adorable. Why did I choose a Rotty? I love them and have since I was a kid. They are playful but an extremely misunderstood breed, made out by the media to be super aggressive. This just isn't the case. As any dog trainer will tell you, it is up to the trainer to work with a dog and channel any aggression they may have in a positive way.

Olive is a lover. We socialized her so well that we only have to work with her on not being so excitable when she interacts with people. She will want to sit on your lap and lick you to death, and does not have a mean bone in her body. Yet, she still is unfairly labeled. My pup is much more than just a family dog. She is my service dog.

During the winter of 2021, my family and I wanted to go out and enjoy some of the festivities going on in a neighboring town. I am not a huge fan of crowds and often would have Olive there because she can calm me down. I was walking down the street with Olive, who was wearing her vest with its Service Dog in Training patch and the insignia of the organization that we were working with. Her vest is bright pink and you can see it from an extremely long distance. In many cases, dogs will bark at Olive and she will not respond. She wags her tail, but rarely engages. When she engages, it is typical sniffing and excitement. Rottweilers have what is known as the "Rotty Rumble.". What is this? When Rottweilers get excited, they will make what sounds like a growl, but if you pay attention it is a little rumble in their chest indicating that they are wanting to play, with tail wagging and ears up.

Because of Olive, I am always aware of my surroundings and who is there. I pay attention to all of the other animals, people, and environment that surrounds us. On this particular brisk December morning, we were excited to head off to the Christmas bazaar. The event was mostly outside, so I thought that it would be a perfect time to bring Olive out for some training with crowds. As we approached the first building, there were two little dogs on the sidewalk. I walked slowly with Olive, giving her the command to heel and stay by my side. Olive is a very playful pup and wanted to play, while these two small dogs, about the size of a men's size 12 shoe, were barking directly at Olive and causing a scene while Olive remained silent. I was used to that kind of behavior with other dogs, so I wasn't alerted yet. We continued to walk down the street and numerous dogs barked at her. She would wag her tail and whimper excitedly. This is a common occurrence and we've learned to deal with it. Things were going well until we reached our final destination.

At the end of the street, where the bazaar ended, there was a concert and a large crowd gathering near a park. Streets were blocked off for pedestrians and different food vendors. Aware of where we were, I made sure to stand on the periphery of the crowd. In my experience with Olive, as long as we gave people space, we never had any issues. Of course, I wouldn't be writing this if everything had gone smoothly. As Olive and I were sitting there talking to some friends with my daughter by my side, a city official came up to me. He had a nervous look on his face. I was nervous because I didn't know him. My hyper awareness of the situation grew and my body started to feel numb. Why numb? This was my nightmare. I was singled out of the crowd and as this man approached me, the crowd started to stare at me. My heart sank and I instantly had a fight, flight or freeze response. The man didn't ask about Olive. He didn't notice her patches designating her as a Service Dog in Training. There was no attempt to talk to me about any issue or situation. What happened? He kicked me out of the event. I was so confused and hurt. What did we do wrong? How come we got singled out when there were so many other dogs barking? In that very moment I felt as big as a wrinkled raisin being kicked off the sidewalk. I was so embarrassed. My body started to tremble and a mild panic attack occurred. In a matter of what seemed to be moments, I was back in our vehicle.

    We were asked to leave because other people felt uneasy with my dog, a Rottweiler, because she was "rumbling." She was not barking or lunging toward any person. She was wagging her tail and wanted to play just like all of the other dogs there. The difference? Her breed and society's fear of that breed. By law, I don't have to disclose anything about my disabilities. The law also states that unless an animal is causing harm or is aggressive, they cannot be restricted from using a public space. We were on a public street, outside of the crowd.

My entire world shifted. I was experiencing discrimination and so was my dog. In the next few weeks, my anger grew because I was so confused about why we were treated the way that we were. I contacted the training group that Olive and I were a part of and they suggested we meet with the man who kicked us out of the event. My wife encouraged me to do it, but I was sick to my stomach about facing that man. Within a month or so we had a meeting scheduled to discuss the event with the city official.

My emotions were running high heading into the meeting. I went there with my wife and a representative from my veteran dog training group. Our goal was to provide information to the city so that this wouldn't happen again to a person with hidden disabilities or any disabilities. The meeting started off with us explaining what a service dog was and what the law is when dealing with a service dog. Despite that, the city official didn't seem to understand where he went wrong. We continued to explain, but at that moment, I lost my cool. I stood up very angry and said, "This dude just isn't getting it," and was ready to walk out. My hands were shaking. My breathing was fast and my chest was beating heavily. Sweat trickled down my back and forehead. Anxiety was at an all-time high. In a matter of 30 seconds or so my wife settled me down and I sat back down. I was so frustrated and feeling unheard.

When this happened, the man who we were talking to had a look on his face of fear. I was ready to march out and file a lawsuit against the city. My goal was to be heard, but instead I had the feeling we were only having one-way communication. After some time, and with help from Meredith and a support person, we finally seemed to connect. Our remaining time in the meeting we discussed what should have happened and how to prevent this from happening again.

This event changed the trajectory of how I utilize Olive. Since that event, I rarely take her out to public events or out and about in town. The look and fear that she gets isn't fair. Olive is supposed to bring a sense of calm with me, but since this situation, I just fear taking her out in public. Going through that humiliation again might be more than I can handle. My dog training has been put on hold and I am fearful of how people will perceive us.

Service dogs are not all treated the same. Service dogs all have a different purpose, but the goal is the same: help the disabled person in any way that they can. This looks very different to some, but it is imperative that we as a society can look beyond the breed and communicate before any negative action, like what happened to us that December day, is taken. Not all service dogs are "service dogs", and I am more than aware of that. I get extremely irritated when I see someone with a service dog that is utilizing the rights of someone disabled, and lying about it. In an interview in November, 2018, with David Griggs, he spoke at great length about his situation with his service dog. He, too, recognizes that there are a lot of "fakes" out there. "Unfortunately there are people out there who are taking advantage of this including people going online and buying a vest and IDs to travel with their dogs on the airplane," said Griggs. " Well yeah, they're misrepresenting a service dog, but in my mind it's worse that, they're misrepresenting a person with a disability and that makes our lives very difficult."

    Add a service dog that society deems aggressive and that adds another layer that makes everything much more difficult for some of us. I am not naive to think that my Olive could be intimidating, but that isn't my fault, nor hers. She does what she is trained to do: recognize that I am having a bout of PTSD symptoms, put her weight against me as a reminder she is there. My PTSD added to my severe anxiety can make some days extremely difficult. Olive and many others get chastised for being themselves. Just like those of us fighting with our hidden disabilities, she is getting judged because of society's perception of her.

Since the winter event, I have not taken her out to the big crowds. I am more worried about what people will say when she is out than the task that I am doing. Because of this, my ability to handle some of the public situations I am in is much more difficult. When you see me interacting with people outside of my family, at times I feel like dying inside. Over time, I have learned how to not shut down, but it is much harder when I am speaking to people I don't know. Once I get to know you, I am more at ease.

Part of this book's mission is to normalize aspects of hidden disabilities. This includes those people who assist disabled persons and service animals. They are doing a job and ultimately are an extension of that disabled person.

Amy reached out after I sent a message on LinkedIn. After speaking to her about her experience, I wanted the world to know about how a stroke affects mental health. Her story is real and you would never know what she has gone through just by looking at her.

Amy Lynn~

It's been almost two years, I don't remember what it felt like before the stroke.

What's normal for me now, is very different from two years ago. January 8, 2022, my daughter was born and my husband and I were absolutely in heaven. January 9, 2022, it was around 5 AM when the nurse came into our room to prepare myself and the baby to go home. You see, my son who just turned seven was home waiting for us and he was very anxious for me to come home. He had been worried that something bad would happen to me while I was in the hospital and I wanted to go home as soon as we could so he could see that everything was fine. After my IV was removed from my left arm, my shoulder and arm on my left side felt funny and soon it spread to the entire left side of my body. Normally if something was odd I probably would've kept it to myself, but for some reason I figured I should probably tell the nurses, especially when my arm felt so heavy and my vision was affected. I felt weird and I was terrified. Shortly after, I was sent to ICU without my husband and daughter and then transferred to another hospital alone.

It was 24 hours after my stroke when I was notified at the hospital that the tests confirmed it was an Ischemic stroke affecting my right thalamus.

I spent the first year postpartum at home with my new daughter healing and it was harder than hard. I desperately wanted to be the mom I thought she and our son deserved while being terrified of having another stroke and being overcome with anxiety and depression like I'd never felt before.

I attended occupational therapy to regain strength and reduce pain, I attended counseling weekly and had more doctors appointments than I'd ever had before.

Healing from a stroke, especially postpartum, was a lot.

Thankfully, the kids needed me which gave me a reason to get up everyday.

I later started seeing a psychiatrist and was officially diagnosed with extreme anxiety, major depressive disorder, PMDD, and later ADHD. While this was also a lot, I felt very validated that there was a reason for how I was feeling. I didn't recognize myself anymore, I was trying so hard to pull my weight at home and not put extra on my spouse's shoulders, but I was being devastated by what was happening inside me. These hidden disabilities.

Meeting new people now, they have no idea I've had a stroke, they are often surprised when I mention it and say, "you don't look like you've had a stroke!"

No, I don't. Thankfully 95% of the physical damage caused by the stroke has recovered.

For the most part, mentally I'm feeling better but the fatigue will always be there, the sensitivity to sound will always be there, fear and depression around health will always be there.

Learning to live around these limitations has taken time especially because they are unseen.

"You only are free when you realize you belong no place - you belong every place - no place at all. The price is high. The reward is great."

"I belong to myself. I'm very proud of that. I'm very concerned of how I look at Maya. I like Maya very much."

~ Maya Angelou

~Amy Hoerle

On The Mound

From the dawn of time, people have admired people who participated in physical competitions, dating back to the days of the Romans and the battles in the arenas. Spectators have longed for the action, the excitement, and most of all, entertainment. What some of those spectators don't see is what happens behind the scenes. The training, the time commitment, the work that it takes to compete at a high level is significant. What else don't they see? The utter abuse that can be associated with sports, which has been around for so long that people have now justified it. Yelling and belittling athletes is extremely common in every aspect of athletics.

During the early 1980's I jumped into the world of athletics. I was interested in every sport that I could play. I started out playing soccer, basketball, football and baseball. I then dropped soccer because it conflicted with football. I played sports throughout my childhood and didn't stop playing until my 30's when my body started to break down.

On the subject of abuse in sports, I want to get something clear: I am not blaming any coaches, but I believe it's critical to address different styles of coaching. Yelling, in most forms, comes in as negative communication. There is truly a difference in putting kids down versus bringing them up. Yelling to make someone feel less than themselves is negative. Punishing the athlete for mistakes in a game shouldn't be a reason to make them feel worse than they most likely already do. The athletes won't ever learn while getting yelled at.

    During my athletic career, I experienced playing with some amazing coaches, but also had some that were flat out abusive. I was always under pressure to perform at the highest level and, at times, that pressure resulted in extreme anxiety and fear. When I played baseball, for example, I was a pitcher and all eyes were on me. Every mistake was noticeable. Every error that I made was in front of everyone. Despite this, at the end of the day, I loved baseball and pitching in the spotlight.

    Baseball wasn't the problem, it was the toxic high school coach that ruined it. It got so bad senior year that I eventually quit halfway through the year. I often look back on that and wonder if it was the right decision, but regardless, that coach had put us through the ringer. He had been coaching for decades and won district and state titles. I grew up with him always watching my performance and as little as eight years old, he was grooming me to be his ace on the mound. As years passed, I got more attention and was throwing the baseball very hard and was having great success on the field. That success carried over to high school and I couldn't wait to start pitching against even tougher competition.

Before the season starts, pitchers are supposed to come in and pitch throughout the year to keep our arms/shoulders loose. I found this to be super fun because I loved the game and wanted to be the best I could be. The varsity coach was an old-school coach and used intimidation as a tool. Miss a pitch on the outside? You were running. Curveball comes in flat? Running and getting yelled at. He expected perfection and would only play those he perceived were trying to achieve it, and yelled at and belittled the players. I threw so much during the next three years that by the time I was a senior, my arm hurt every day during practice. I lived on a bag of ice and constantly applied sports creams to help with the pain.

During my junior year, we were doing workouts in a dimly lit gym. Pitchers were throwing to each other and took turns being the catcher. I was always worried about doing this, but the coach didn't care. My vision was less than perfect and the gym was very dark. My friend at the time and I were pitching together during a session. One of my biggest fears happened. I misjudged a pitch and the ball hit me square in my left big toe. It instantly was on fire and I knew it was broken. I walked up to the coach and told him what had happened. He responded in an angry tone, "So you are going to be out? Are you sure it is broken?" He didn't believe that it was broken, while I was devastated about the injury. I wanted to play so bad that rather than having the doctor perform surgery, a hard cast was put over the cleat. I had a spider break and the pieces of bone were essentially shattered. Within a week I was back out on the mound. I fought through the pain because I was afraid of losing my spot due to the injury. I played on it during the entire year while it healed incorrectly. In a few short months after baseball was over, football season was going to begin. I didn't want surgery because I knew I would be out at least eight weeks. It wasn't until after football season that I got the surgery done—a toe fusion with a titanium screw placed in that toe, and the knuckle was gone.

During that baseball season I pitched well, but not up to the standard that the coach wanted. While growing up and going to his baseball camps, he would tell me I would be a Division-1 starting pitcher one day. My love for baseball never wavered, but I started to doubt my ability. This was due to the coach constantly giving me negative feedback. I didn't know it then, but I was suffering from Imposter Syndrome.

Imposter Syndrome: Noun

1. anxiety or self-doubt that results from persistently undervaluing one's competence and active role in achieving success, while falsely attributing one's accomplishments to luck or other external forces.

Junior season ended and I was getting ready for my senior football season. My senior year playing baseball was going to be *my* year. I had worked at this sport for 14 years and was hopeful to play in college, as I'd been told my entire life by this coach. I had surgery on my toe right after football season. This gave me plenty of time to heal while also doing exercises to strengthen my arm and shoulder. When my toe healed, I got started on winter workouts. In the gym at 5:30 in the morning working on my mechanics. The coach was on me constantly and often asked if I wanted to be a starter. If I missed a pitch or a location, he just shook his head in disapproval. As a team, we never felt supported. The season started and things got so bad that I ended up quitting halfway through the season. This coach was notorious for yelling so aggressively that spit would shoot out of his mouth. It was like a toxic work culture, except it was sports.

This period caused everlasting memories and heartbreak and at the time, I thought it was all my fault. Years later I realized it wasn't me. The coach created a culture of negativity through mistreatment of so many players over the years. Interestingly enough, this is a pervasive problem with sports today.

Never will I say that all coaches are bad because they yell. It's not that they are yelling, it's what is being said. I was once told by a coach, the minute I stop being on you is when I don't care anymore, which is a very confusing statement for a kid. I'll never forget one of my coaches. He was my 8th grade basketball coach and probably the best coach I ever had. What he did that was different from so many other coaches was that he would get upset with something and teach us how not to do the thing anymore. That approach generated results and we won the league that year. Good coaches are inspiring and care about the health and mental health of their athletes.

These behaviors can be extremely harmful to anyone, not just the athletes. People are heavily influenced by the leaders who they associate with. Molding starts as soon as five years old playing youth sports. Coaches have a tremendous amount of power to change the life of our youth. This is a responsibility that should be common sense, but unfortunately this isn't the case.

Just recently, my daughter's volleyball coach and staff have shown how a coach can be intense, but not toxic. As of now, all of the squads (four of them) are undefeated and the varsity is ranked top in the state for all schools in Washington. During practice and games they are professional and positive. During one of the matches, the head coach had a disagreement with a call on the court. She remained calm even though she was upset. After a discussion with the judge, he ruled for the other team's favor. Her response? "I don't agree with the call, but I respect your decision." That is what it is all about—leading by example. It's not like this coach is a pushover either. Practices are intense and intentional. When they make a mistake, it is a conversation, not a punishment.

How does this translate to mental health and hidden disabilities? I'll give an example. There was a day when my daughter was having a very difficult day at school. She called me to pick her up and did not want to go to practice. I had her stay and talk to the coach before leaving. After speaking to the coach while having tears in her eyes, the coach told her to go home and take care of herself. This is how you prevent mental issues stemming from sports. Compassion and empathy should be required qualifications of any coach.

I had the chance to interview the head varsity coach from Prairie High School in Vancouver, WA. This program represents how coaching and teams should be. Her coaches all have the same motto and their program has the success to show it's working. She has experience in coaching and playing at all education levels and was a Division 1 volleyball player in the Southeastern Conference.

Jen Palmer~ High School Head Volleyball Coach

My coaching style has changed over the years, and is now one of the things I am most proud of. While growing up as an athlete, I played a lot of different sports, and had a lot of different coaches. As I got older, I narrowed in on the sport in which I was the most passionate about, volleyball. There are two coaches that really made a positive impact on me growing up. I felt like they genuinely cared about me as a person. I felt heard and seen by them, and knew my worth regardless if I was a starter in the lineup or not. These two individuals were unfortunately the exception, and not the rule in my athletic journey. I had a lot of coaches that I really struggled with. I had a hard time respecting their way of communication, and therefore I had a hard time respecting them. I struggled a lot with my self-worth, confidence, and continuously compared myself to others. Some coaches that I had did not help to cultivate a safe and loving environment, and I was by no means inspired by them. My teammates did that for me. I was lucky enough to play with the most incredibly talented and hardworking individuals. They helped to teach me resilience, and pushed me emotionally and physically. Luckily, I was able to create my own healthy relationship with the sport I loved, and later was able to fully understand the impact a coach can make, both positively and negatively.

      I started coaching volleyball once my collegiate career was over. I wanted to find a way to stay in the gym, because I was still in love with the game. I missed the competition, being a part of a team, and loved the opportunity to still be able to jump on the court and play. There is a greater meaning of the word "coach" now, as I start my 17th year. Maturity, experiences, motherhood, and mentors have all played a significant role in my coaching style evolution. When starting as a head varsity coach at my current high school, I was lucky enough to learn from amazing people. I continuously welcome other coaches to share their knowledge with me so that I can continue to learn and grow in the game, but with these mentors I learned more valuable lessons from them that had nothing to do with our sport. These mentors of mine taught me that the most valuable thing I could ever give to an athlete is love and genuine care. I entered a program with them called 3-Dimensional Coaching, and it completely changed my approach. It opened my eyes to so many opportunities, and taught me just how influential I could be, and the power my position can hold. 3-Dimensional Coaching highlights three main dimensions of an athlete, and by eliminating just one of these dimensions from your coaching focus, could leave the athlete not reaching their full potential. The physicality, psychology, and heart of the athlete are all equally important factors to attend to. By utilizing this 3D framework, it has allowed me to be completely intentional with each individual. A lot of coaches coach the game and not the athlete, which was my focus when I first started as a coach. I am so grateful to have been surrounded by people that encourage me to be the best version of myself that I can be. As I continue on that journey, I am proud that I have selected like-minded people that are willing to join me in that mission by being more focused on relationships. With that mindset, in the end, we all win.

As a coach, we have a huge responsibility. I don't think we could ever try to guess how impactful we could be in a child's life. Some athletes may spend a short time thinking of our influence on them, while others may send letters or wedding invitations years later. I have had the privilege of receiving both of those gifts, and it's an incredible honor, and a reminder of how important a meaningful adult relationship can be in those teenage years. We also never know what personal struggles the child is facing at home. In 17 years, I have been a part of some very heavy conversations, and been privy to a lot of personal family information that have been heartbreaking. Some athletes are facing abuse at home; verbal or physical, suicidal thoughts or attempts, bullying at school (or around the clock, thanks to social media), the pressures of feeling they need to work to help their parents with financial struggles, athletes who are the sole childcare for their younger brothers or sisters, or have substance abuse issues they are personally facing/or that surrounds them etc. As passionate as I am about volleyball, it is just a sport. Sports lead to so many other intrinsic qualities and dozens of benefits, but it is still just a sport. As a coach, I ask myself, what am I doing every day that will stay with this person once their athletic career is over?

     I am not a perfect coach. I have so much passion and intensity, and that oozes out of me. I am also one of the most competitive people I know; growing up with older competitive brothers was partly to blame for that I think. Sometimes, I wish I was more composed. I am an open book, and my emotions are written on my face. I don't demand perfection, but I expect 100% effort, and require respect. In a program where we have to cut almost 40 kids, it is a privilege to make a team. How would it be fair to the athletes that did not get to participate each season, if I were to allow these athletes in the program to not appreciate the opportunity? It would not be fair to the varsity athletes to let them coast through this season without demanding themselves to be pushed out of their current comfort zone, both physically and mentally. These athletes play club volleyball year-round and have collegiate aspirations, and it's my job to push them to be better players and teammates every day. I raise my voice, and speak passionately about this sport we share. There is a difference between yelling AT them and yelling FOR them. My intensity and passion toward an individual are a direct reflection of my relationship with them and love for them. I have built relationships with these girls over the years, and they know my heart and my intentions. I have never belittled, disrespected, sworn at, or put one of my girls down. However, I think showing passion and intensity channeled respectfully toward our goal is a great thing to exemplify. It is okay to teach and expect respect. It is okay to redirect a teenager when they have made a poor choice. It is okay to let an athlete know that you want to see more from them. All of these things are not only okay but, in my opinion, a duty of ours to the next generations so long as we go about it the right way. As a role model, it is necessary that we give much more of those things to them than what we ask for from them. We need to show them respect, honesty, integrity, and productive communication. We are influencing these kids to be better *humans, it is more than the game. All of the lessons of hard work and respect carry well past this season, and their high school career. When the foundation of my relationship with that athlete is strong, and they know the love and care for them is there regardless of their performance in a game, I know that I am doing my part in helping this student athlete; both in the game of volleyball and the game of life.*

Athletic discipline to me is reinforcing the physical or mental expectation of the team's system. Coaches can reinforce this in several ways. I like to communicate what was done, what needs to be corrected, and then have the athlete participate in repetitions of the corrected movement/behavior. When I think of negative discipline, it sounds like a punishment; having the athlete receive a consequence for an action that is not connected to the area of concern, or does not lead to the outcome that is desired. When it comes to team dynamics in this area, I think there is a significant difference between playing disciplined vs playing fearful. Negative discipline can make an athlete lose confidence, joy, and ultimately make them fearful of making a mistake. I want my athletes to serve tough, or swing hard on game points. Mistakes are part of the game, losing will absolutely happen, but the lesson in failure is the most important part of it all. I will always tell my athlete to "Go for it!", "Trust yourself!". If they do that, and the point doesn't swing in our favor, it's a loss that is worth taking, and I would bet that that mindset and their confidence will come through next time when it matters most, and that confidence will continue with them off the court.

As a player, I never had a hard time associating discipline with having fun in my sport. I knew that discipline=success (winning a lot of the time), and winning=fun. It was always a simple equation for me. Coaching a varsity team, I am surrounded by more of the same like-minded individuals, than perhaps our 4th team in the program. I have found the bigger obstacle is trying to get the athletes to understand the cause and effect of the little things that they decide to do or not do. Having discipline in just the little things can make a good team great. For example, when we have a defensive base on the 10 ft line, it is not disciplined to go stand on the 11ft line. Getting an athlete to understand that it's more than just a difference of a foot, it is a bigger picture than that, is one of our goals.

My practices consist of several different components every single day. We do daily conditioning as an entire program. I do believe that you can 'condition' in drills, but I have found a ton of value, mostly with the younger teams, for this to be a program wide activity. During this time, we *encourage support and cheering for each other, regardless of the team they are on. We enforce discipline and integrity, having an extra rep if an athlete did not do the first one correctly, and so on. After conditioning we have a daily ball handling sequence, where with their partner they count their reps of a specific instruction, and try to beat their score from the day before. This is monotonous, but has so much value. More often than not, the team with the better ball control will win. These drills do not excite them, however when consistent, over time the athletes will see the benefit of doing them, and in turn will create buy-in, at which point the discipline becomes easier. Athletes love to compete, so I have found that it is extremely beneficial to create competitive games that encourage focus on whatever specific detail we are trying to enforce. Just recently, my amazing assistant coach came up with a volleyball drill, where it is essentially a game of Tic Tac Toe. It is a 6 V 6 game where one side has to earn a point off of serve receive two times in a row. If one side does that, they receive a 'free-ball', if that point is won, that team then gets to place a specific color cone on our (athletic tape) tic tac toe board. This continues until one team has accomplished three in a row. This is motivating for the girls because it is fun, but it also serves our purpose in having their focus be to side-out with intent when we are the receiving team. As a coach, I* always want to see my players have joy, otherwise why would they continue to play? It is my goal to always create a positive environment where athletes can be pushed, experience success and failures and learn from them, and ultimately experience joy throughout the entire process.

    I am sure a lot of coaches measure success differently. In college, I was a freshman 6 rotation starting setter at a D1 school in the Southern Eastern Conference. On my recruiting visit I was told they were in a rebuilding year, and to expect to come in and help to lead. After a very short time it was very apparent that our success, in the terms of wins in the season, would be limited. Coming from a high school team with 8 teammates who played D1 post high school, and two state championships my junior and senior year, it was a huge adjustment. While working through this adversity, and adjusting to life in college a couple thousand miles from my home and support system, my college coach told our team that his livelihood was at stake, and it is our responsibility as a team to start winning to make sure that he was able to provide food on the table for his family. While I don't approve of his method of motivation, I can understand the point he was trying to make now. As a high school coach, my paycheck is minimal, and I do not do this for the money. In my 8 years at this high school, I have had 3 incredibly supportive athletic *directors. While I have several league titles, district placements, and state trips and trophies under my belt as a coach, my win/loss record has been by no means indicative of my overall success or job retention.*

At the high school level, I have two huge focuses, build skill and build character; the latter is the most important to me. Helping to develop good people is the very most important thing, and the area in which we put the most emphasis on. I am so proud to feel like we are a top tier program in class, respect, and integrity. We help to cultivate this environment by making sure this is exemplified from the top down. As leaders we take this responsibility seriously, and know we are being watched by many impressionable minds.

In addition to setting a good example ourselves, it is just as important to be clear in expectations on and off the court, and communicate them up front, clearly, and often. Communication is one of my greatest strengths, and it has helped me be successful in all areas of my life; with my children, with my husband, with friends, and in my professional endeavors. Efficient communication can help to alleviate any conflicts that could arise in the future. I love the parents in my program. There is a long-standing comment in the coach's world about how parents can make or break an experience for coaches. I have had several conflicts over the years with parents, and I have learned from every one of them. Reflecting on my time as a younger coach, I can completely envision how a different approach in my communication could have helped the outcome be a more positive one. As I have grown in many areas, I have the confidence and self-awareness to handle any questions or conflicts that come my way from parents or athletes. I know that at the end of the day, the majority of parents want to know that their child is being respected, cared for, treated correctly, and benefiting from their time in the program in some way shape or form. If a parent is not happy with playing time, for example, I can at least rest peacefully at night knowing that I am giving this athlete much more than what the parents may feel is missing. Communication with my athletes is imperative. My athletes know my expectations on and off the court, they are clear and concise. It is important that once these expectations are established, there is no faltering in the follow through of the previously communicated consequences of not meeting these expectations. These consequences need to be known prior, consistent, fair, and applied to everyone regardless of what is at stake. Consistency is key in maintaining respect from my athletes. Putting emphasis on having good character, being respectful to teachers, parents, refs, coaches, and teammates is a constant focus. We make sure to let our athletes know that we care and will give attention to more factors than their performance on the court; it transcends to the classroom and their home. When their grades are suffering, there are conversations and support put in place. When we are told by teachers of disrespectful behavior in the classroom, there are conversations, apologies given, and consequences and accountability that is transferred to the court/their team. As coaches, we work with the high school staff and parents to help this athlete be the best version of themselves they can be.

Another measure of success is the pure joy that can be seen on the court. Watching them come together to accomplish a common goal is one of the best things to witness. My varsity team this season has struggled to play consistently at their level, without the 'roller coaster' of ups and downs; both mentally and physically. I have been hard on them, being vocal when they play down to their opponents' level. Making it known that our goal is to beat our own performance each time we step on the court. After several team talks without much change, I decided to do something different. I communicated that the next time we are not playing to our potential (regarding the things that are always 100% in our control- attitude and effort for example), that I was going to continue to coach, but that I will give the athletes more of a voice to step up and ask more from their teammates, instead of having me be the one that is constantly asking more from them. I cannot make them want it, it has to be decided on their own. One match, the first set was way too close, and we were not playing disciplined. I coached the game, but did not coach the mental side and waited. After set 1, my captains respectfully asked if the team could have a meeting in their huddle without coaches. My coaches and I smirked at each other, as if silently thinking "finally, it is happening!". Set 2 and set 3 was a drastic change. They played with intent, so much joy, and a lot of discipline. It was a game changer. From that moment on, we have played like a different team, a team that in the last two weeks have been able to purely focus on the physical strategies, without the need to be asked to work harder or talk louder. Just last week we played a big successful school, and lost a tough one in 5 sets; our first loss of the season. The pretty amazing part is that I would take that losing team last week over the winning team of the previous weeks. My team, against our huge opponent, was disciplined, fiery, joyful, determined, and fearless. I had goosebumps watching them rise to that challenge, and I could not have been prouder of their performance, and their heart.

    When I walk away from coaching, I want to reflect on the relationships I have built and truly feel that I have made a *positive difference in the lives I was a part of. I want to know that I did my best to exemplify class, integrity, high moral character, empathy, honesty, passion, and genuine care. The success of this program can be seen in many ways, and that gives me such a great sense of pride. We have been successful on the court. Not only by the standards of our win/loss record, but by the small wins we see daily. Just last week one of our 3rd team girls who has struggled with conditioning, was beaming with pride after pushing herself to her max and making her sprints under the timed goal. That was a bigger win for her than we probably even realize. These small improvements make a big impact on the confidence of these young girls. Those small wins add up, and it is fun to see the huge improvements made over the course of the entire season. It teaches them that with hard work, comes great reward.*

I love what I do, and am so thankful that I can confidently say that I understand the weight and importance of this role that I play in these children's lives, and will continue to strive to do right by them,

because they deserve it.

~Jen Palmer

Now, in my 40's with kids of my own, I think back to the days of playing youth sports. We accepted and never challenged the coaches who were too extreme. Coaches were treated as if they were gods. People of power. Who dared to challenge that? I told myself when my oldest kids started to play sports that I would not allow coaches to undermine my children or other children. I have had to have some stern conversations with some coaches, but I wasn't going to allow my kids to experience lasting trauma from playing. Sports are supposed to be fun. That doesn't mean that there are no rules and discipline, but the way that those situations are handled make all of the difference.

At the end of the day, the percentages for playing sports in the professionals are slim to none. Youth coaches should be coaching more than the sport, but how to be good fundamental humans. Being competitive doesn't come from being yelled at and made to feel down. Youth coaches should be more like educational teachers and carry themselves with the same standard. Good athletes will be good athletes regardless of who is coaching them. When the yelling and abuse starts to happen the athlete will lose respect and in many cases, end up quitting a sport they loved solely because they are tired of the coach. Change is slowly happening, but it is going to take new coaches to have empathy and think bigger than just the sport.

Current State of Mind

The truth is that I am going to struggle with mental health for the rest of my life. I am going to continue to learn how to heal, but the wounds from my past will always be there. This past year, in particular, has been extremely tough and has brought major challenges.

Our family has gone through a layoff, a family mental health crisis, a cancer scare and that doesn't even include my career change. My father has been having health issues and almost had complete liver failure and my mother-in-law was diagnosed with stage three cancer. All of these events have been extremely stressful and we are currently going through all of it.

My son, who is in high school, has had his own battles this year with hidden disabilities. He has always been a unique kid in school and in life. As he was growing up, he loved building things and figuring out how everything worked. He wanted to have friends and always seemed to have a few, but never a big group. Throughout his life, he has battled suicidal ideation, separation anxiety, and severe depression. All of this came to a head this past summer.

For his entire life, almost, he has split his time between living with his mom and me. This was a traditional 50/50 Legal and Custodial split. The exception is when his mom left and I had him full time for two to three years when he was a child. This has been going on since he was about four years old and he never really felt like he had "a home" as we were always moving. During the last part of his sophomore year, he came to me and said that he wanted to move in with me full time. I asked him why, and what was going on at his mom's to make such a large decision, but my wife and I said "of course." We wanted to get in front of whatever he was going through.

It was an intense couple of months and we were monitoring him as best as we could, but any 17-year-old is almost impossible to monitor 24 hours a day. Everything seemed to be going well until we found things he wasn't supposed to have under his bed. This included many cans of alcohol and marijuana cartridges. We always asked him to clean up his room, but he would just stuff things under his bed and in his closet. While looking for a phone charger that he had borrowed, we found garbage and food dispersed throughout the entire bedroom, with rotting food and bugs all over the place.

Obviously, this is not the sign of a healthy teenager. We confronted him about everything that we found and his demeanor completely changed. You could see his emotions tank and his eyes fill with darkness. I was super upset, but wanted to know why this was going on. He burst into tears, and the next thing I knew our world was upended.

My kiddo was facing many demons that night and they all decided to drop in on him at once. He was crying and talking about jumping from his window. To put this into perspective, his window was around thirty feet high above a cement pad below. I had to call the local police because he was acting in a way that I had never seen before. In the past, I was able to hold him and console him while he calmed down. This time was unlike any other and I was extremely scared. The police were extremely understanding and got us in touch with a crisis specialist on the phone for him to speak to. After an hour or two, he settled down.

I slept with him on the couch that night and waited until the morning to evaluate what had happened and what we were going to do next. After we woke, he was not doing well and made the decision to get help. After speaking to him, he said he felt the same as the night before. I suggested that we go to the emergency room to seek help. He agreed. That morning we went to the hospital.

We got to the hospital emergency room and they put us in a hallway that was going to be monitored at all times.

There were four beds lined up with people sitting next to them monitoring each patient. All of the patients were kids on suicide watch. We met with a few specialists as well as a social worker who was evaluating the situation. Twenty-four hours had gone by and the social worker insisted that we got him checked into a short term youth psychology ward.

Shortly, we were off to a clinic to help him for a week-long stay. After picking him up, I thought that we were on the right path. Although he was in a short-stay clinic, the goal was to achieve some positive results that would help him manage his anxiety attacks and depression. During his stay, he was partially diagnosed with depression, anxiety, and possibly high-functioning autism as well as a possible bipolar disorder. All of these conditions, paired with being a 16-year-old, could send anyone into a spiral.

When the decision was made, I took him to the clinic. After about an hour, we had him checked in and ready for the week's stay. I remember looking at him and had so many emotions of guilt, worry and grief. I'll never forget that day. I said goodbye to him, gave him a huge hug, and walked back to my truck. At that moment my world crashed and the flood gates opened. I was almost hysterical because of the deep emotions I was feeling. He was my first born and at the time, I felt like I had failed him somewhere. How could my little boy be so sad and confused? Where did I go wrong? I gathered myself as best as I could with a deep pain inside of me. The thing about mental health and those who suffer from mental health is that it is extremely difficult to see past your own emotions which makes healing so difficult.

I picked him up a week later and hoped for the best. He had agreed to try some medications that would help with his depression and anxiety. After two weeks of trying to help my kiddo, he was not getting better and I was worried. I had to confront him about him taking his medications. Two weeks of being in his room for 22 hours a day, I had to have a talk with him about not progressing. I told him that if he didn't make any progress, I would have to look at taking away a few things. One of the things that I said I was going to take away from him was football. This wasn't because I didn't want him to play, it was because he could have hurt himself, or worse someone else. At the time, he was extremely unpredictable. When he heard what I was thinking, he got up, silently and walked downstairs. Zero words and he wouldn't look at me. As he walked to the front door, I attempted to stop him from leaving. The door opened and out of instinct, he stuck his arm in to stop it and the door slammed against his arm. In a split second, I kicked the door trying to keep him from leaving. The door had fractured the arm. When an event like this happens,

Child Protective Services is always called. They had to open up an investigation, and they agreed that the incident was a total accident. Ultimately, after this incident he wanted to leave and ultimately felt he was going to be better off living with his mom for a while.

This has been extremely difficult for me and tested my own mental health. My son is going through things and at his age, it is almost impossible to know what is truly going on. Society puts so much pressure on teens today that even the good days can seem gray. My hope is that he finds himself over the next few years and becomes the man I know he can be.

Over the course of eight months or so, he is still living with his mom. I have very little communication with him, if at all. When he is in distress, he will reach out sometimes. I always tell him I love him and will always support him. After that, I won't hear from him for a while. This last time, he said he still loves me. Not much more I can ask for at this point.

Going through the teenage years without any major trauma is tough enough, but when you add in trauma, it adds a whole new level. Teenagers can be rough around the edges and being cruel seems to be part of their nature. Observing the classrooms that I am teaching and the peers of my kids, the pressure to be "perfect" is unreal. Everything from their hair, clothes, and the music that they listen to is being judged at all times. The few who are able to express themselves are extremely rare. Adding in any hidden disabilities to the mix can be extremely difficult. These students aren't trying to do anything other than survive.

According to the Centers for Disease Control and Prevention (CDC), "Mental health problems in youth often go hand in hand with other health and behavioral risks like increased risk of drug use, experiencing violence, and higher risk sexual behaviors that can lead to sexually transmitted diseases and unintended pregnancy."

Amidst all of that going on, I was also laid off this year. For many years, I have been involved in technical recruiting and sales. The industries are always wild and most of the time unstable. After years of being laid off and being let go, my wife and I decided it was time for a career change. I took a look in the mirror and decided to finally pursue my childhood dream of being a teacher. This career field is stable and will allow me to spend quality time with my family.

For someone who struggles with mental health, anything can cause them distress, which for many, exposes many of the hidden disabilities that they have and work with day-to-day. Because of my career change, my income has been cut by more than 75%. We have to prioritize many different things now that we didn't before. Spare change? Goes to a bill. It would be easy to go down the slippery slope if I let all of this eat at me. At this point, I will push forward and get through it and come out on the other side.

Beyond that, my father's health and my mother in law's health, this year has been one for the ages. Our parents are getting older and will continue to have health issues arise as the years go by, so I know that keeping a healthy mental balance is going to be imperative for my resilience and avoiding severe anxiety or depression.

Currently, I have a fear of what my parents are going to think when this book comes out. What type of relationship are we going to have? My goal is that this opens up a line of communication so that the healing process continues. We concentrate on what we can control. Look forward, not behind.

A Therapist's Take

When Max reached out and asked that we have a conversation on the book that he was working on, **Hidden Disabilities**, I was curious but was also honored that he wanted to hear my input. It was when I finally had a meeting with him that I realized how knowledgeable, intentional, and passionate he was on the topic. My heart was elated because the area of mental health, especially, Men's Mental Health is an area of interest for me. I resonated with his project, and most importantly, his passion. I immediately saw how I could be part of it.

Since the book is on hidden disabilities, I thought I would share my thoughts on **Hidden Disabilities affecting Men.** But before I continue expounding on the topic, Max asked an important question as the title of his book, **Eyes Can't See.**

To be honest, this question, when I first saw it, took me by surprise! It went past my defense mechanisms, cut through the layers of my soul, and went straight to my heart. All I could think of is that this question is at the **core of every existential crisis** affecting us all, as human beings.

Our core needs, as human beings, I believe are to be *seen, heard, and understood*. And to be honest, this question not only shook me but made me realize one of the things that I have personally struggled with, is to feel seen and my voice to be heard. My colorful personality, bubbliness, spontaneity, immense creativity, warmth, and cheerfulness, are **seen, validated, heard, and allowed to be expressed in a safe, healthy way.**

As I write this, I am thinking of all the ways I have not felt seen, heard, and understood. For example, last week, I was feeling down and discouraged because I have been going through transitions in my life where I have had to let go of relationships that I no longer felt aligned with. As much as it was liberating, and I understand why it had to happen, it is still painful. I have struggled to get relationships where I felt really seen.

Have you ever felt that you are the one who is empathetic, most of the time, to others and those around you rarely see and accept you for who you really are? Do you ever feel like you are the one trying to figure out how to be more accommodating and understanding to others but rarely gets reciprocated?

It is not that they do not do things for you, it is because they do not resonate with your language, and sometimes do not honor and respect your ideas and vision. It was then that I had the epiphany, that I had relied so much on people to see me, that I completely forgot to **see myself.**

And so, as Max asked, Can You See Me? I ask you the question that my personal reflection and contemplation on the subject matter asked me, **Can You See Yourself?**

Can You See Yourself?

As Max has written about Hidden Disabilities, his experiences, and recommendations on what can be changed, I write to men and encourage them that as it has been described, hidden disabilities are those that are not seen by the naked eye, but are very real personal struggles one struggles with and one of them is **hidden mental disabilities.**

Invisible disabilities, also known as *hidden disabilities or non-visible disabilities (NVDs)*, are disabilities that are not immediately apparent. They are typically chronic illnesses and conditions that significantly impair normal activities of daily living (Wikipedia, 2023).

Mental disabilities or illnesses, such as **ADHD, Dyslexia, Autism, or Schizophrenia**, are also classified as invisible disabilities because they are usually not detected immediately by looking or talking to a person.

96% of people with chronic illnesses have an invisible disability. It is estimated that 1 in 10 Americans live with an invisible disability (World Disabled, 2014). This number is likely higher worldwide, as 80% of all people with disabilities live in developing countries (United Nations Enable, 2023).

As someone who has been diagnosed with depression and ADHD as a young teen, I can tell you how real the struggle is. Hidden mental disabilities or mental health issues are real and need a lot of help and support in managing them.

One of the hidden mental disabilities that men go through is **trauma or PTSD. Trauma** is an **emotional response** to a terrible event like an accident, rape, or natural disaster. Immediately after the event, shock, and denial are typical. Longer-term reactions include unpredictable emotions, flashbacks, strained relationships, and even physical symptoms like headaches or nausea (APA, 2023).

Post-Traumatic Stress Disorder (PTSD), on the other hand, is a **psychiatric disorder** that may develop after a person has experienced, seen, or been threatened with a traumatic event. One of the people who experience this hidden mental disability is **male veterans.**

I believe that one of the **underlying causes** of male depression is **unhealed or unresolved trauma**. Repeated exposure to trauma, from a young age, over time, becomes too much to bear and when one is not able to find safe places to vent, heal, and be, then it becomes **C- PTSD** which is also known as **Complex -Post Traumatic Stress Disorder**. Experts across the field of psychology disagree on whether C.P.T.S.D is a **distinct condition and diagnosis.**

At the end of the day, many male veterans suffer in silence and end up taking their own lives, from these hidden disabilities. It is said that veterans are **1.5 times** more likely to **die by suicide** than nonveteran adults. Reasons for these sobering numbers may include high exposure to trauma, stress and burnout, isolation and loneliness, easy access to and familiarity with guns, and **difficulties reintegrating into civilian life** (DeAngelis, 2022).

If you are a male veteran, and you are reading this, I would like to say that what you have experienced, in life and in service, we may not fully understand. The pain, anger, and grief from your experience in service may be beyond words and may feel impossible to carry. But I would like to remind you that *you are a hero.* Your service was not in vain and it is not too late to seek help and support as you experience this hidden disabilit(ies)y.

Support is available, and it is possible to heal. Yes! Very possible. And I will share with you some of the strategies that may help you in your journey to recovery and most importantly, journey back to your **authentic self** which you may have felt disconnected from for such a long time.

I believe that it is **possible to heal and prevent suicide**. I would know because I am healing every day. Or at least I am **intentional** about reclaiming my health. I believe you could too. Some of the strategies I recommend include but are not limited to:

- Going for **individual, group, couple (if in a relationship), and family psychotherapy sessions. Why is this important?** Because it will help you not only heal yourself, but it will help you foster healthy relationships with others, and have a sense of community and team building that is essential to **health and longevity**. As the old adage says, "*No Man is an Island.*" Men need communities too. A community of fellow brothers, mutual understanding with your spouse or partner and good relationships with your children or those that you are responsible for. Sometimes building and maintaining relationships with others can be daunting, especially with hidden mental disabilities, but with the right kind of help, support, and understanding, your relationships can truly thrive. That is why **psychotherapy** is a good place to start. So why not start today, **right now**? Seek a professional psychotherapist within your area and reach out.

- **Eating healthy foods.** Intentionally eat a diet that is rich in vegetables, legumes, whole fruits, healthy fats like olive oil, avocado, nuts and seeds, whole grains such as whole meal bread and brown rice, and finally good quality protein from eggs, poultry, fish and some red meat (in moderation) and legumes like beans, peas, and lentils. These are some of the examples of foods that are good for your mental health as a man, but for best results, consult a **dietician or nutritionist.** The foods are not only good for your mental health but are known to improve **overall health and longevity.**

- **Exercise.** I know this word is often associated with going to the gym, and that is okay and healthy as long as it is moderate and consistent. I would like to introduce new insight here and mention that exercise not only means going to the gym, but it actually is a **natural movement**. You not only get to enjoy it, but it is effective when **consistent**. An example would be, instead of driving every day to work, you choose to walk, jog, or cycle to work. Instead of taking the lift, why not try the stairs?

Going for runs more and perhaps instead of doing it alone, you do it with your fellow male friends and make it a contest, just for fun! There are countless ways to get the job done. Exercise doesn't have to be a 'yucky' thing you dread, but you can incorporate small ways of doing it differently. As you do this, you will notice your life and perspective begin to broaden which means yay to your mental health!

Ps: I have nothing against the gym. If it works for you, keep going!

- **Purpose or Ikigai.** *Ikigai* **(ee-key-guy)** is a Japanese concept that combines the terms *iki*, meaning "alive" or "life," and *gai*, meaning "benefit" or "worth." When combined, these terms mean **that which gives your life worth, meaning, or purpose**. As a male veteran, you may have experienced different changes and transitions when in service. You may have even been trained to handle those sudden changes and transitions and in as much as it was difficult getting tasks done, you managed anyway. But when it came to **transitioning back to civilian life**, you may have been **underprepared** and when life didn't unfold as you perceived, it caused panic. The traumatic experiences came flooding back into your psyche when the threat was no longer there, but you were now in a relatively new environment and what you were feeling didn't make sense. And so the symptoms worsened, and sometimes those around you weren't ready for the person you are now.

I want to say that **trauma is often a normal response to an abnormal situation.** It is normal to have those emotions and it is a shared experience with other human beings around the world. What I would recommend is not only seeking professional help but also **finding new purpose and meaning.** Ask yourself, how can I help humanity with the pain and trauma I have experienced? How can I turn my pain into purpose? How can I turn my pain into *power*? That question **holds the key** to helping you not only **heal the world but also heal yourself.** I realized, in my personal human experience, that when I help others when I am stuck, **I help myself.**

Pain is a teacher. Pain has a purpose.

Feel and express it in a healthy way by helping others, for example through **volunteering or starting a business** that helps others heal what you went through, and your world, and the world will never be the same again.

This actually reminds me of something, I just thought of adding here as a **bonus** tip. I have been exploring the issue of **wealth and purpose** and I noticed that they are closely intertwined.

Healing is becoming Wealthy (Health is Wealth). Wealth is a spiritual practice.

It's probably no surprise that worrying about finances can cause or increase stress, anxiety, and other mental health issues. That could be especially true for veterans who may already be dealing with post-traumatic stress disorder (PTSD), depression, physical injuries, and a loss of connection after military service. Add financial woes to the mix, and it can be a slippery slope. According to WWP's (**Wounded Warrior Project**, an organization dedicated to helping wounded veterans) Warrior Survey shows that financial strain on warriors/ veterans has increased since 2021. In 2022, more than 6 in 10 warriors (64%) reported that they did not have enough money to make ends meet at some point in the past 12 months (Wounded Warrior Project, 2022).

Financial Health is a very vital aspect and often neglected area that affects mental health. I realized this when I had an epiphany a few months ago that I needed to change how I viewed money and wealth so as to not only be better in my personal finances and businesses, but also have better mental health. Money has always been a great area of pain for me and like I have shared, pain is a teacher. I had to come to terms with my financial situation if I wanted to make peace with it.

Uncovering my financial trauma made me realize that a healthy relationship with money was connected to my *sense of identity and purpose*. If I wanted to experience financial peace and ultimately good mental health, I had to face my worst fears which are rooted in my sense of worth. This is a scary practice because it uncovers a lot of difficult emotions such as shame, guilt, anger and fear but with the help of a therapist, you are able to uncover the root of these "ghosts" and resolve them once and for all.

When this happens, you find a new sense of peace within and that uncovers areas of potential within you that generate wealth and ultimately good mental health. Hence my quote, **Healing is becoming Wealthy (Health is Wealth).**

Wealth is also a spiritual practice because it is tied to your **sense of identity, worth, purpose**. Once that is uncovered, you get to help others which can be in the *form of a business or work* that generates healthy profit. For example, I am using my difficult experience with money (experiencing money wounds and trauma) to help people in my practice as a *Wealth Therapist*. I believe you can do it too. Help is available! And you are more resourceful than you know!

- **Be Authentic.** The final tip I would personally recommend is to **be authentic**. The journey to authenticity often involves the **journey to consciousness**. *Authenticity and consciousness go hand in hand.* I would like to encourage you to reconnect with yourself, your *childhood dreams,* and reconnect with your *masculine essence.* Whatever way that means for you, I encourage you to do it.

Why?

Because **your healing is connected to your authentic self.** As long as you are not connected to your authentic self, you will continue showing up as someone else, which is exhausting and is not good for your mental health.

I would like for you to take a moment to envision yourself, *where you are now and the person you would like to be.*

Do you like what you see? Good! Then keep that image with you everywhere you go, because, that, my friend, is **your own hero.** It is not too late to evolve to that image. I don't care if you are 65 or 80, it is not too late to reconnect with your true self.

Your authentic self is what unlocks your personal legend which is your ideal image, which unlocks your purpose. And when you unlock it, congratulations! You unlock your sweet spot, you become unstoppable and hence leave a legacy of helping other people reconnect with themselves as you did for yourself. **Do not give up.** This is the time to **buckle up** and enter *Phase two, four, six, eight* depending on where you are in life. Your life begins again now! The question is, will you take up the challenge? Will you go on this new adventure that is beckoning you? Will you say yes to a new life? It is all up to you!

As I conclude, I want to encourage you to do just **one thing** today. **Just one**. One from just reading this book that will take you closer to your *personal legend*. I will not ask for much.

You may not be a male veteran yourself, but you may ask yourself what you can do so that your friend, family member, spouse, or even neighbor, can feel *seen, heard and understood*. I would encourage you to ask them what they may need to feel supported. And when they share with you, do the best you can to help them transition into becoming a civilian again. It may take time, but if you learn to be patient with each other, *beautiful relationships are bound to be formed* and evolve over time. No true relationship evolves without **conflict**, but as long as it is healthy conflict, you can both work through it to make life better to not only support those who struggle with hidden disabilities but learn to have beautiful relationships with them. As they receive support, they are bound to feel safe and adjust to their new lifestyle more easily. They end up being the most thoughtful and caring members of society because they learn to appreciate support given to them. And don't we all, as human beings wish to experience such? Don't we all appreciate when people were kind to us when things were emotionally tough for us?

Remember, **you and I can only extend love and kindness to those who need it when we learn to first extend it to ourselves.** *We can only give to the degree and measure we learn to give ourselves.* As we support male veterans, or even all people living with hidden disabilities, let us also remember to engage in **self- care, go for therapy and have a support system** too. We are all human beings. Let us remember to fill our love cups (by speaking our love languages to ourselves) as we support those who may need our support in difficult times of need.

Hidden disabilities may be a struggle, they may seem like a hindrance, but they could be a *blessing in disguise*. The world is constantly looking for people who will never give up, overcome all odds and challenges set up against them, and make it to the finish line. The world is looking for heroes who will rewrite their story and give it the best ending. *Or at least die trying.* The world is looking for **authentic souls** that despite many challenges like hidden disabilities, will still rise, *be a light,* and show others that **It- Can- Be- Done!**
It is too expensive to give up!

The world needs you and like they always say, there is indeed no one like you because *we are all unique* and have personal unique stories to tell.

Originally,

Maryanne Wanjiru Kibuchi,

Trauma-Informed Wealth Therapist.

Beyond the Cover

Over the years I have been in some dark places. I have battled many demons and will continue to push forward. Ever since childhood, for almost 30 years, I had been abused in one way or the other. Everyone thought that I was always happy and confident. Bottom line is that I never truly was. I was always worried about going home. I was afraid of asking questions for fear of the response I would get.

What many people don't realize or understand is that people can appear to be okay on the surface, but the careless actions of others could be killing them inside. Many mental hidden disabilities are caused by some sort of trauma. It can start as early as birth. A lot of kids are so used to what is going on in their life, that they don't understand it is going to affect them years later.

Physical hidden disabilities were not talked about, but I wanted to address them. The expression "don't judge a book by its cover" couldn't be more true. Let's just break down an example. I am a 100% disabled Veteran. People assume that if you are 100% disabled, you should show those things. That isn't what 100% is with all injuries combined at different rating levels. Example: A veteran has a disability percentage for migraines, low back pain and shoulder pain. Each of those conditions have a disability rating percentage. If those are all percentage over 100%, then the veteran is now a 100% rated veteran. Just because the veteran isn't with a limp today, doesn't mean that tomorrow they will be walking with a cane. Now, does that equal 100% all of the time? No it does not. Then how is that 100%? There may be times where the veteran is expressing pain and symptoms all at the same time. That is 100% because all the ailments are present at the same time. This confuses many people when they hear about our percentage. I have spoken to several 100% rated veterans and most of them you could never tell.

Claire Szewczyk breaks this down and explains it in detail.

Your entire body is equal to 100%
You have three rated conditions:

- The first is a back injury rated at 30%
- The second is a knee injury rated at 20%
- The third is tinnitus rated at 10%

You would think that the combined rating would be 60%, right? 30+20+10%? Nope, that isn't the case.

First- you start with the largest rating, your back injury at 30%. That rating is subtracted from 100%

Now, of your total body, 70% remains.

So, now instead of subtracting 20 for the knee injury at 20%, you can only subtract 20% from the 70 that is remaining! Which is 14 (0.2 x 70 = 14). 70 – 14 = 56.

Now, for the last 10% tinnitus related, you again only subtract 10% of what is left of the total body. At this point it is 56 (from the last step), so (0.1 x 56 = 5.6) 56 – 5.6 = 50.4.

Now the combined rating is 30% + 14% + 5.6% = 49.6% (which you would round to the nearest 10). So, 50% total disability.

They appear to be fit, strong, and looking like there is no way that they are 100% rated. That is the problem. People judge by our looks, but seldomly look past what they can't see.

For parents and future parents: remember that everything you do will be remembered. What you do in front of your children, fighting, yelling, and physical abuse will cause more harm than you can ever imagine. We have talked about the after effects of the abuse, but it needs to hit home. In my family growing up, an event happened and there was not a time where we would discuss what happened. As a youth, I had so many misconceptions about what I experienced. Multiple years where my depression and anxiety grew. As an adult, I am taking the power back and learning to accept what has happened, but continue to find a way to move forward without resentment.

    This book isn't targeted towards anyone, the military, coaches, parents or any of those who have been brought up. If you think this is about you, that is a problem. If you are angry, take a look in the mirror. Abuse is abuse no matter what age a person is. That abuse causes lasting images. Those images are burned into the memory bank. Currently, people are using Psilocybin Therapy to help with previous trauma. Some folks have remembered trauma from their childhood. They are discovering more about themselves and understanding how to deal with previous trauma. The work to recover is truly never over. The feelings of fear and depression will come and go. Remember, mental abuse causes so many problems that in the moment, you don't realize it. I am not laying blame on those who have hurt me in the past, but I am writing this book to provide a perspective about people with hidden disabilities.

Psilocybin Therapy:

    A promising form of guided Cognitive Behavioral Therapy using the psychoactive substance of psilocybin that researches suggest may have the potential to treat a wide range of mood and substance disorders

"Our findings add to evidence that, under carefully controlled conditions, this is a promising therapeutic approach that can lead to significant and durable improvements in depression," says Natalie Gukasyan, M.D., assistant professor of psychiatry and behavioral sciences at the Johns Hopkins University School of Medicine.

How can you be an ally to those with hidden disabilities? One, if you feel you have done something that has caused harm to someone in the past, acknowledge what happened. Don't gaslight them. It doesn't matter what age the person is that was abused. Even though the damage is gone, it will make the abused person feel better when you address it and apologize. The hardest part of this is facing the truth and that is very hard for some. They might feel ashamed of what they have done, but damage is damage. The abuse happened.

With all this said, this doesn't mean that those people with hidden disabilities didn't have any good times. This means that the damage and abuse will be traumatic for the majority of their life. Empathy and compassion for people with hidden disabilities is extremely important. Just because you can't see inside someone, doesn't mean that they are not struggling. In many cases the person with hidden disabilities won't tell you that they have any disabilities. Being a person with a hidden disability is tiring at times. Why? Because when you look a certain way, seemingly healthy and put together, people have a hard time understanding why you are disabled. We, as people with hidden disabilities, have to answer many questions of the how and why. It becomes part of your life. In most cases, the person with hidden disabilities will suffer from them for a lifetime. There is no escape from it. Just finding a way to deal with it in whatever way works.

For me, it took until I was 37 years old before I was at my breaking point. I needed help and was on the verge of suicide. All of those hidden disabilities came rushing forward all at the same time. My own family had no clue I was feeling so bad. After speaking to a counselor, we developed a plan to help. It has now been three years of therapy. During therapy, I had to find out and discover why I was always in a confused state because I didn't ever look inside. The layers of the onion started to peel back and vivid images from my past now surrounded me. How did I get to a stable place? Well, there is no truly stable place, but this book, whether it helps or not, has been an outlet for me. I know that I will always struggle with my hidden mental disabilities, but I am learning how to deal with them in a safe way.

Over the last few years on this mental health journey, I have learned so much about the severity of hidden disabilities that I do not have. Listening to so many people talk about their experiences has helped me realize that we are not alone. Just because society can not see what we are going through, but we know others are struggling just like us. One of the many goals for this book that I want to accomplish is spreading good information on this topic.

There are so many people that I talk to who have no idea what hidden disabilities are. I have been in front of people of all ages and often ask the same question when subjects come up, "How are you 100% Disabled." They can't see it, making it difficult to realize or understand. Over the course of writing this book, it has become abundantly clear that this topic has been neglected. I am here to change that.

Take this book with you. Share it with a friend. I am going to share it with the world. Let's do this together and implore people to know they are not alone. Mental health matters, even with the people you least expect.

Acknowledgements

Editors-

    Debra Perry

    Helen Townes

    Meredith Traughber-Crismon

Forward-

    Azlan Allen

Contributors-

    ABE3 Tom

    Lucas Velmer

    Jen Palmer

    Mike Lee

    Suzie Schweitzer

    Fred Melvin

    Amy Hoerle

Mental Health Expert-

    Maryanne Wanjiru Kibuchi

    Trauma-Informed Wealth Therapist

Cover Design-   Robert Robbins

    Charles Sandoval

Thank You!

I have to thank so many people for the help with this book. It was a long hard journey, but I am happy with how this turned out. This was accomplished from guidance from those who know more about writing than I do.

I wanted to spotlight one person in particular. She has given me guidance and mentorship for over 25 years now. When I first started writing this book, I had one person in mind to help with the editing process. This just happened to be my high school English teacher, Debra Perry. Everything had come full circle. I was lucky to have Debra as my teacher twice and she sparked the writer in me. I enjoyed writing papers, poems and a few other things. Writing let me escape and gave me an escape into another world.

Then, in high school English, we had a creative paper we were supposed to write. I could not tell you what the prompt was, but I know that I put my all into it. The words flowed onto the paper. At that time, I was learning how to put more depth into descriptions. Pulling the reader into the story and writing in a way that the reader could see what they were reading as if it were real. That was the paper that Debra pulled me aside in class and talked to me about what I had written.

I'll never forget it. It was one of the first times in school where I felt like I was able to achieve something academically. I'll never forget what she said, "Max, you are going to be a writer some day". That was all it took for my confidence to grow.

That was over 20 years ago and although I have written a variety of things here and there, this book is the largest writing project I have ever written. Most people have a favorite teacher or professor. Ms. Perry was mine. My spark lay dormant for many years, but it still burned inside. I just had to figure out what I was going to write. Thank you, Ms. Perry, even though she has told me many times to call her by her first name!

Thank you, Ms. Perry, for believing in me and always being in my corner clear into adulthood. I don't know if I will ever be able to thank you enough or let you know how much of an impact you had on me. The world needs more humans like you!

I also wanted to thank my wife, Meredith. Over the last few years a lot of self-discovery has happened. Grace was the first person to really listen to my trauma and help me face it after all of these years. There were many times that she encouraged me to go to therapy, but it took a long time to get there. I was afraid of opening up old wounds and facing the demons that I knew that I would face.

Today, I am a better man and have a better sense of clarity because of the support of Meredith. Things are not always easy, but she has stuck through all of the challenges. She is my wife, but she is also my best friend and number one supporter on so many levels.

REFERENCES

1. American Psychological Association (APA,2023). **Trauma.** Retrieved from https://www.apa.org/topics/trauma#:~:text=Trauma%20is%20an%20emotional%20response,symptoms%20like%20headaches%20or%20nausea.

2. DeAngelis, T. (2022, November 1). **Veterans are at higher risk for suicide. Psychologists are helping them tackle their unique struggles.** American Psychological Association. https://www.apa.org/monitor/2022/11/preventing-veteran-suicide

3. "Factsheet on Persons with Disabilities **"United Nations Enable"**. www.un.org. Retrieved 2 July 2023.

4. Invisible disability. (2023, November 7). *In Wikipedia.* https://en.wikipedia.org/wiki/Invisible_disability

5. Krouse, L. (2022, June 27). **What is Post Traumatic Stress Disorder (PTSD)?** Verywell Health. https://www.verywellhealth.com/what-is-ptsd-5084527

6. World, Disabled (1 January, 2014) **"Invisible Disabilities: List and General Information"**. Disabled World. Retrieved 2 July 2023.

7. Wounded Warrior Project (WWP, 2022). Retrieved from https://newsroom.woundedwarriorproject.org/How-Financial-Worries-Can-Affect-Veterans-Mental-Health

Made in United States
Troutdale, OR
03/30/2025